TRACING YOUR FAMILY HISTORY

ROYAL NAVY

compiled by Allison E Duffield,
edited by Sarah Paterson

IMPERIAL WAR MUSEUM

ISBN I 901623 36 X
2nd Edition

CONTENTS

PREFACE

Day in, day out – and for many years past – rather more than a third of all the public enquiries received by the Museum's Department of Printed Books staff have concerned family history. In many cases we answer these using our knowledge of military history and military institutions and with information from our own rich collections. However, we can also provide accurate referral to the many sources and contacts we know, both elsewhere in the Museum and at scores of other specialist institutions and resources far and wide. The details change over time and new sources emerge. We have to keep up to date with these developments if we are to maintain the quality of our service. With the *Tracing Your Family History* series we aim to share our knowledge with you, helping you to find and understand the information that is available. This second edition of *Tracing Your Family History: Royal Navy* does just that. It has been comprehensively revised with all the latest information that we ourselves use in our enquiry work.

We are grateful for all the advice and help we have received from Museum colleagues and from other organisations in the preparation of this guide and its predecessor.

Richard Golland
Keeper
Department of Printed Books

ABOUT THE MUSEUM

One of the founding principles behind the establishment of the Imperial War Museum (IWM) in 1917, was its function as a collective memory. Although the original plan for listing the names of the fallen as an intrinsic part of the building never materialised, the Museum has always regarded the individual and his or her experience as being of paramount importance. In his opening address in June 1920, Sir Alfred Mond 'the father of the Imperial War Museum' declared the hope that the collection would be made *'so complete that every individual, man or woman, sailor, soldier, airman or civilian who contributed, however obscurely, to the final result, may be able to find in these galleries an example or illustration of the sacrifice he made or the work he did, and in the archives some record of it.'* Consequently, today we can offer a wealth of material to the family history researcher.

A walk around the main displays on the major conflicts of the century at the Museum in Lambeth Road can help provide a context for a relative's service. There are also additional branches at Duxford in Cambridgeshire, HMS *Belfast*, moored on the Thames opposite the Tower of London, the Churchill Museum and Cabinet War Rooms off Whitehall and Imperial War Museum North in Manchester.

The scope of the Museum encompasses all twentieth century conflict, concentrating on the British and Commonwealth involvement since 1914. In an age of total war, every family in the United Kingdom has been affected in some way. The study of family history, perhaps boosted by the greater availability of information on the internet, has grown considerably over recent years. From schoolchildren interviewing grandparents to local historians writing commemorative histories, the burgeoning growth of this popular activity has made it a real industry. Many of the individuals engaged in research can learn much from the material housed at the Imperial War Museum – original art works and objects of war, personal letters and diaries, contemporary film and photographs, retrospective recorded interviews, and the invaluable collection of printed materials, journals, maps and ephemera. Research may be done in any of the reference departments of the Museum – the Departments of Art, Documents, Exhibits and Firearms, Film and Photograph Archives, Printed Books and the Sound Archive. Access to these collections is both welcomed and encouraged, although a prior appointment is usually necessary. Initial approaches can be made by telephone, letter or e-mail, and staff can provide advice about how to proceed with an enquiry and what materials might be available.

For the family researcher, the first port of call will generally be the Department of Printed Books. This constitutes a national reference library containing well over 150,000 books and pamphlets, 30,000 journals and an impressive range of individual maps and ephemera items, such as ration-books, propaganda leaflets and song-sheets. It is important to stress that the Imperial War Museum **does not** hold any personal service records or official documentation, although through both this booklet and our normal enquiry service, we can offer advice on what and where remaining sources may still be found. We do have a wide range of items in our collections which will assist the researcher. These can all be consulted under one roof, with experienced staff on-hand to direct and answer enquiries.

The primary aim of this booklet is to help the enquirer find out about individuals who served in the Royal Navy. Some basic information is given in the following paragraphs, and useful book titles which will help those unfamiliar with the subject, are given in the bibliography at the end. All of these titles are held by the Museum and can be consulted in the Reading Room, but for those unable to make a personal visit, full publication details are given to enable other copies of the books to be ordered through the public library system. Addresses of the various institutions which may assist can also be found listed in Appendix IV.

Strenuous efforts have been made to ensure that the information contained in this booklet is accurate. If any errors have inadvertently been made, we would appreciate it if these could be drawn to our attention so that amendments can appear in later editions.

HOW TO USE THIS GUIDE

Tracing a naval ancestor is a quite different experience from that of researching an army relative. A major advantage is that the service records for both world wars are largely intact. However, establishing exactly *where* they are held may not be so easy – especially if you are unsure whether a relative came under the jurisdiction of the Royal Navy, Royal Naval Reserve or Royal Naval Volunteer Reserve (more detail on these distinctions can be found in Appendix I). Once the service record is retrieved, postings and movements are well documented and an outline of a naval career can be established at a relatively early stage in the research.

Although published ships' histories can be extremely helpful, coverage is not comprehensive and the search for original documentation and ships' logs may form a vital part of your research. The service or technical establishments ashore tend to be less well documented than the ships and men who constituted the 'front line'. Even so, the Museum has much to offer and, beginning with the Department of Printed Books, we can both direct you to the appropriate official documentation and provide references to technical, historical, autobiographical and other published sources.

Firstly, if you have no precise details of the individual's career turn to the section on **Service Records**. This section attempts to explain which records can be found at which address. We have tried to provide as accurate a statement of holdings as possible, and much time has been spent researching this material, but the situation is subject to change and flux, with a large number of records being prepared for removal to

The National Archives (previously known as the Public Record Office). If you know very little about the structure and organisation of the Royal Navy or are in doubt about which branch your relative served with, you will probably find it helpful to read Appendix I in conjunction with this section.

Tracing medal citations can be difficult. The section on **Medal Records** provides some explanation of the different classes of medals awarded and directs you to some of the better books on the topic. Please note that it is not always possible to trace citations for all gallantry medals.

It is usually easier to trace those who died than those who survived their war service. All sailors and naval personnel who died in the two world wars are recorded. The section on **Casualty Records** describes the key sources available, both published and unpublished. Full medical records giving information on wounds and medical treatment are not generally available centrally, although where treatment was provided on board ship or at a naval base this information may be noted in some of the later service records. Local sources and published rolls of honour for schools, firms and so on, can sometimes provide unusually detailed information.

The appendixes are designed to be dipped into as required. Appendix I gives a brief outline of the Navy's organisation, hierarchy and chains of command. Details of recommended titles can be found in the **Select Bibliography** in Appendix V. No bibliography can be comprehensive but we recognise that guidance to some of the best and most appropriate works can save the researcher valuable time. The key addresses mentioned in the text have been repeated in Appendix IV, together with contact details, where available.

We hope that this guide will ease your way into the naval world and wish you every success in tracing the information you require.

SERVICE RECORDS

Pre-First World War naval records can generally be found at **The National Archives, Ruskin Avenue, Kew, Richmond, Surrey TW9 4DU**. The National Archives was formerly known as the Public Record Office.

It is worth noting the existence of the new-style *'Service Register'*, introduced alongside Continuous Service in 1853. From that date every rating was allocated an official number, which he retained throughout his service. At discharge, his career was summarised and a record compiled, showing time spent on each ship. This detail was recorded in his service register, which was filed by his number, (see Appendix II for a fuller description of the official numbering system). Service registers relating to officers were arranged alphabetically by name. Registers contained details such as date of birth, marriage and death, information on pay and pension, and reports by senior officers. This information forms the basis of the service record.

Before pursuing more detailed information and background on an individual's career, it is useful to confirm as many details as possible by accessing the official personal data available. No published listing is available on the service career of ratings. However, editions of the *Navy List*, published continuously from 1814, are the obvious starting point for any search into an officer's career, as they contain seniority lists of all officers, cross-referred to individual ships, which in turn list their complement of officers. Included are retired and Reserve officers in employment, together with yard and civilian officers, Women's Royal Naval Service, Queen Alexandra's Royal Naval

Nursing Service and other Admiralty officials. During the First and Second World Wars much of the usual information was omitted from the published editions of the *Navy List* and confined to confidential editions for 'service use' only. A full set is held by The National Archives, but the Department of Printed Books holds a near complete run, including many of the confidential editions, for the period 1914 to date.

As has been stressed earlier, the Imperial War Museum has no official unpublished documentation relating to service. However, detailed below are a number of official archives which may be of assistance. Please note that many of the archives listed will only release information to either the serviceman or woman concerned, his or her next of kin or a legal beneficiary. However, information may be released to other interested parties who have prior consent from the individual concerned or their next of kin. In most cases search fees will be levied. Enquirers are recommended to put their requests in writing, quoting in full the name, and as much factual information as is already known on the rank, number, unit and service of the individual concerned. If no details are known, some basic information may be available from the *Absent Voters Lists* of 1918 and the *Service Voters Registers* of 1945, compiled in order to enable servicemen to vote in the constituency of their home address. These should be held by the relevant local library, town hall or county record office. The entries often contain details of address, unit, number and rank.

Another potential source of information is the **Family Records Centre, 1 Myddelton Street, London EC1R 1UW** which provides research facilities previously provided at St Catherine's House. Their records include indexes of births, deaths and marriages since 1837; legal adoptions since 1927; and births, deaths and marriages of some British citizens abroad since the late eighteenth century.

Many of the relevant records relating to naval genealogical research are still held by **Ministry of Defence** departments and agencies. Genealogical enquiries must be made in writing. You may have to wait for a reply as the Ministry of Defence's principal function is to respond to official enquiries concerning welfare, employment, pensions and other legal matters. The basic search fee is currently £30.

Any personnel records that are no longer restricted will be held by **The National Archives (TNA), Ruskin Avenue, Kew, Richmond, Surrey TW9 4DU**, where they are available to the general public. In principle, personnel records are transferred to The National Archives from the Ministry of Defence departments when they are 75 years old. Thus most First World War and immediate post-1918 records are now on open access. It is possible that records may be held in more than one location – for example if your relative served in both the First and Second World Wars, you will probably need to source different parts of his service record at The National Archives and through the various Ministry of Defence departments and agencies. Class *ADM 340* at The National Archives contains some information about officers and their service from the 1880s until 1960.

The National Archives has produced invaluable guides to their holdings in the form of published handbooks and a series of records information sheets and leaflets, which can be accessed directly via their web-site at **www.nationalarchives.gov.uk**

Of particular note are *Tracing your Ancestors in the Public Record Office*, 6th edition, edited by Amanda Bevan, *Naval Records for Genealogists* by NAM Rodger and *Tracing your Naval Ancestors* by Bruno Pappalardo.

The **Fleet Air Arm Museum, Centre for Naval Aviation Records and Research, RNAS Yeovilton, Yeovil, Ilchester, Somerset BA22 8HT** in some instances holds the originals of records that have been microfilmed for The National Archives, as well as some complementary materials. These records mostly relate to ratings. An appointment with the Centre for Naval Aviation Records and Research should be made in advance of any visit. Contact details can be found in Appendix IV.

The following listing by branch of service gives details including the location of restricted access files:

ROYAL NAVY

Officers' records for the First World War and some confidential reports are now available, on microfilm, at **The National Archives**. Admiralty files *ADM 196* contain details of executive and warrant officers' entire careers. There is no overall name index to these records; they are arranged by the dates of commission and seniority. These dates can be confirmed from the *Navy List*. Admiralty files *ADM 340* may also be helpful.

Records of Royal Navy ratings who enlisted before 1923 can be found at **The National Archives**. See the *Registers of Seamen's Services* in Admiralty files *ADM 188*. Index volumes are also available.

The **Fleet Air Arm Museum** has holdings of the engagement papers of Royal Navy ratings, serving between 1888 and 1923.

Records of executive officers whose service began after 1917, of warrant officers whose service began after 1931 and of ratings in service from 1924 are currently held by **Navy Search, TNT Archive Services, Tetron Point, William Nadin Way, Swadlincote, Derbyshire DE11 0BB**, together with the records of those regular officers and ratings in service up to 1950.

For service records covering 'Hostilities Only' service from 1939 (ie those taken on solely for service during the Second World War and Korea), and of those regular officers and ratings in service after 1950, please write to **DPS(N) (Directorate of Personnel Support (Navy)), Building 1/152, Victory View, HM Naval Base, Portsmouth, Hampshire PO1 3PX**.

ROYAL NAVAL RESERVE

Records of Royal Naval Reserve officers in service up to 1920 are now available in the Admiralty files *ADM 240* at **The National Archives**. These records provide details of merchant as well as naval service and are arranged in order of rank and date of seniority. See the *Navy List* for ranks, dates of commission and seniority.

Details of officers in service from 1929 until 1950 are still held by **Navy Search**. The records of those serving after 1950 are held by **DPS(N)**. Some information should be available at **The National Archives** in Class *ADM 340*.

Records of Royal Naval Reserve ratings in service during the period 1914-1958 (including the First and Second World Wars) are also now available at **The National Archives**. See the Board of Trade files *BT 377* held on microfiche and arranged in service number order. Name indexes are also available.

The **Fleet Air Arm Museum** also has the original records of Royal Naval Reserve ratings from 1908-1955.

Information on ratings who saw service after 1958 is held by **DPS(N)**.

Although the **Royal Naval Reserve Trawler Section** was set up as a separate section for the duration of the First World War, service records are included with those of the Royal Naval Reserve at **The National Archives**.

Records of those who served in the **Royal Naval Patrol Service** during the Second World War are held by **DPS(N)**. Since Sparrows Nest, Lowestoft became the Central Depot for the Royal Naval Patrol Service in 1939, family historians will find some additional material at the **Lowestoft and East Suffolk Maritime Museum, Sparrows Nest Gardens, Whapload Road, Lowestoft, Suffolk NR32 1XG**.

ROYAL NAVAL VOLUNTEER RESERVE

Records of Royal Naval Volunteer Reserve officers in service during the First World War (and up to 1922) are now available in the Admiralty files *ADM 337*, at **The National Archives**. These records are accessed by a card index.

Records of officers in service between 1923 and 1958 are still with **Navy Search**, thereafter at **DPS(N)**. Some information should also be found at **The National Archives** in Admiralty files *ADM 340*.

Records of Royal Naval Volunteer Reserve ratings in service during the First World War (up to 1919) are also in the Admiralty files *ADM 337* at **The National Archives**. These records are arranged by Division (eg London Division) and then by service number. If this information is not already known, you will need to check in *ADM 171*, the Medal Roll.

Ratings' records for the period 1920-1958, like those of officers, are with **Navy Search**, thereafter at **DPS(N)**.

If no records of service can be found it may be worth contacting the **Fleet Air Arm Museum** as they hold a selection of engagement papers for Royal Naval Volunteer Reserve ratings. Again, as these are arranged by service number you will need to know this before a record can be found.

ROYAL MARINES

Records of officers up to 1925 are now held at **The National Archives** in the Admiralty files *ADM 196*. An index to these files, covering the period up to 1970, is in *ADM 313*.

Records of other ranks are arranged according to the Division and Company to which a Marine belonged. Service records up to 1925 are now held by **The National Archives** and are to be found in Admiralty files *ADM 159*, with a selection of records in *ADM 157* and *ADM 158*. An index to these files is also contained in *ADM 313*.

Some Royal Marines attestation papers (dating from the 1850s to the mid 1920s) can also be found at the **Fleet Air Arm Museum** (although these are principally those for Marines from the Plymouth and Chatham Divisions; there are very few from Portsmouth).

Please note that Royal Marines' files are subject to a 75-year closure period. All enquiries concerning any Marine enlisted less than 75 years ago should be addressed to **DPS(N), Building 1/152, Victory View, HM Naval Base, Portsmouth, Hampshire PO1 3PX**.

ROYAL NAVAL DIVISION

The Royal Naval Division was a unique formation consisting of sailors serving on land as infantry. Most of the men came from the Reserves, although there was also a Royal Marines Brigade. In 1916, the Division transferred from Admiralty to War Office control and was renamed the 63rd (Royal Naval) Division (it also acquired an Army Brigade and various military elements). However, Royal Naval Division records were treated quite separately and are accorded their own files. These are now available, on microfiche, at **The National Archives** in the Admiralty files *ADM 339*. Generally speaking, the records of the men of the Royal Marines who served with the Royal Naval Division can be found in the holdings for the Royal Marines, whilst the records for the Army men can be found under the War Office.

The **Fleet Air Arm Museum** also have good holdings of enlistment papers relating to the Royal Naval Division.

ROYAL NAVAL AIR SERVICE AND FLEET AIR ARM

Records of officers who served in the Royal Naval Air Service during the First World War are to be found at **The National Archives** in Admiralty files *ADM 273*, for which there is a card index. Please note that no details are given regarding officers' previous Royal Navy service (see *ADM 196*) or subsequent Royal Air Force service (see *AIR 76*).

Similarly, records of ratings who served in the Royal Naval Air Service during the First World War are in the Admiralty files *ADM 188* at **The National Archives**. For those who served with the RNAS Russian Armoured Cars, 1915-1919, see Admiralty files *ADM 116*. As with the officers, subsequent Royal Air Force service is recorded in *AIR 79*.

Records of those who joined the Fleet Air Arm during the period 1924-1938 are held by **Navy Search**. Records of those who saw service during the Second World War and beyond are still held by the **DPS(N)**.

The **Fleet Air Arm Museum** holds copies of records similar to *ADM 273*, engagement papers of some Royal Naval Air Service personnel who did not transfer to the Royal Air Force, and officers who enlisted as ratings but were later commissioned, in their **Centre for Naval Aviation Records and Research**.

The **Royal Air Force Museum, Grahame Park Way, Hendon, London NW9 5LL** can provide copies of the Certificate Record cards and, in many cases, photographs of Royal Naval Air Service pilots who trained at civilian flying schools.

COASTGUARD

During the twentieth century the Coastguard Service has been administered by many different departments: the Admiralty, Board of Trade, Ministry of Shipping, Ministry of Transport and Department of Trade. Records of this Service are therefore scattered between files for these different formations at **The National Archives**.

Service records of Coastguard officers, 1886-1947 are in indexed Registers in the Admiralty files *ADM 175* at **The National Archives**. Discharge Registers for 1919 are included. In addition, references to all aspects of the Coastguard Service are in the Admiralty files *ADM 1* and *ADM 116*. Other useful classes include *ADM 120, BT 166* and *BT 167*. Although these chiefly contain administrative files and papers, some include details of individuals and of particular Coastguard stations.

WOMEN'S ROYAL NAVAL SERVICE

The National Archives holds the records for the Women's Royal Naval Service (WRNS), covering the period 1917-1919. Records for those with officer status are in the Admiralty files

ADM *318* which includes an index arranged alphabetically by name. In addition there are two registers of appointments, promotions and resignations in ADM *321*. Records for those who served as ratings are in the Admiralty files ADM *336*, arranged by service number. There is an index at ADM *336/1-22*.

Records for WRNS who entered service between the Second World War and 1955 are held by **Navy Search**. Later records are held by **DPS(N)**. You should find some information for WRNS officers who served in both World Wars in Admiralty files ADM *340*.

Family historians may also be interested to learn of the *WRNS Collection* at the **Royal Naval Museum, HM Naval Base (PP66), Portsmouth, Hampshire PO1 3NH**. Although the Collection has more material from the Second World War than from the 1917-1919 period, it does hold the original ratings' enrolment forms from the First World War.

QUEEN ALEXANDRA'S ROYAL NAVAL NURSING SERVICE

Records of Nursing Sisters, who entered the service before 1929, including Queen Alexandra's Royal Naval Nursing Service (QARNNS) Reserves signed up for wartime service only (1914-1919) are in the Admiralty files ADM *104* at **The National Archives**. These files are indexed, arranged by dates of appointment and include service details up to 1959. Included in ADM *104* are nursing establishment books, 1912-1927. Nursing staff stationed at individual hospitals and barracks are listed by date of entry.

Records of those serving with the QARNNS after 1929 are held by **Navy Search**. Records of those who joined the service from 1956 are at **DPS(N)**.

VOLUNTARY AID DETACHMENTS

Records of Voluntary Aid Detachments in service during the First and Second World Wars are held by the **British Red Cross Museum and Archives, 44 Moorfields, Moorgate, London EC2Y 9AL**. In addition some information on VADs and their service during the First World War is to be found at **The National Archives**. See the Ministry of Health files *MH 106* and the Admiralty files *ADM 104*. Naval VAD records dating after the mid-1940s are likely to be held by **Navy Search**. In 1960 Naval VADs ceased to serve, as Queen Alexandra's Royal Naval Nursing Service introduced auxiliary ratings.

MEDAL RECORDS

Campaign medals were awarded for taking part in a particular campaign, or for service in time of war. Often a 'clasp' was added to the ribbon of these medals, to denote a particular campaign, eg 'Minesweeping 1945-51' on the Naval General Service Medal. The clasp was also used to denote second or subsequent awards of Long Service and Good Conduct medals.

These medals can be a useful source for researchers as, during the First World War, they usually included the name and unit details of the recipient, engraved either on the rim, or on the back of the medal. Unfortunately, during the Second World War, as an economy measure, campaign medals were not stamped with these details although arrangements could be made to have this done privately.

For more detailed information on the medals themselves and the range of the awards available please refer to the publications listed in Appendix V. Those with internet access may also be interested in the Imperial War Museum's web-site **www.iwm.org.uk/collections/exhibits/ex-medal.htm** which provides details of First World War campaign medals.

Many of the records relating to campaign medals and gallantry awards are available for public consultation at **The National Archives**. Microfilm copies of the original card index for the recipients of campaign medals of the First World War, including the 1914-15 Star, British War Medal and Victory Medal, together with large bound volumes of medal rolls, are to be found in the Admiralty files *ADM 171*, for which some index volumes are available. There is a separate group of files for each medal.

The original cards were arranged alphabetically by the surname of the recipient and included their initials, unit, rank and number. Medals for women serving under Admiralty command can be found in *ADM 171/133*.

Although **The National Archives** holds some medal rolls for the period after 1921 in the Board of Trade files *BT 164*, (eg awards to Royal Naval Reserve officers for the period 1939-1946), in general, records for this period are lodged at the **Armed Forces Personnel Administration Agency, MOD Medal Office, Building 250, Royal Air Force Innsworth, Gloucester, GL3 1HW**. Campaign medals for the Second World War are the 1939-45 Star, the Africa Star, Atlantic Star, Burma Star, France and Germany Star, Italy Star, Pacific Star, the War Medal and the Defence Medal.

The **MOD Medal Office** also deals with medal claims and/or replacements (although these will only be issued under stringent conditions). Medals may only be issued to the recipient or, if deceased, to the next of kin. It will also be necessary to provide official documentary proof of entitlement.

Gallantry medals, first instituted in the middle of the nineteenth century, were awarded for a particular act of gallantry. The addition of a 'bar' to the medal ribbon of the original medal denotes a second or subsequent award for gallant or distinguished service.

No medals were awarded for **Mentions in Despatches**, although a certificate was issued. Recipients were authorised to wear a multi-leaved oak leaf emblem on the ribbon of the relevant campaign medal. After 1920 the emblem changed to a single oak leaf.

The amount of information available on these awards, varies considerably. Notification of an award would normally be published in the *London Gazette*, sometimes accompanied by the citation (a short description of why the award was made). However, there was often a considerable delay between the date of the award and the date that the notification and/or citation were published. It should also be noted that, even though an individual may have been recommended for a particular medal, it may not have been granted, or a 'lesser' award may have been substituted. Please note that at the beginning of the Second World War, publication of all citations for gallantry awards was suspended and that no citations for Mentions in Despatches are available *for any period.* All enquiries regarding citations for naval gallantry awards not published in the *London Gazette* should be referred to the **Naval Secretary (Honours and Awards), Victory Building, HM Naval Base, Portsmouth, Hampshire PO1 3LS**.

The Department of Printed Books holds a near complete series of the *London Gazette* from 1914 but unfortunately, without a complete set of the all-important indexes. However, **The National Archives** holds a full set and researchers may also find copies in some of the larger reference libraries in their area.

The *London Gazette* (as well as the *Edinburgh* and *Belfast Gazettes*) is now available on-line, and you can check the awards of gallantry medals, promotion of officers or the naturalisation of a relative by using the web-site **www.gazettes-online.co.uk** The Historic Archive contains First and Second World War issues only (1914-1920, and 1939-1948).

The Admiralty files *ADM 171* also contain references to gallantry awards for the period 1914-1921, including references to Mentions in Despatches. Many members of the Royal Marines and the Royal Naval Division were given Army gallantry awards, and some Fleet Air Arm personnel were given Royal Air Force awards. References to these are to be found in the War Office files and Air Files at **The National Archives**.

For records of awards made after 1939, apply to **Naval Secretary (Honours and Awards)**.

Details of women who received honours and awards are recorded in the Admiralty files *ADM 104* as well as in *ADM 171*. The listings in the War Office files *WO 162* are also worth checking.

Procedures for gallantry medal claims and/or replacements are the same as those outlined previously for campaign medals. Recommendations for gallantry medals from 1914 are to be found in the Admiralty files *ADM 1* and *ADM 116* at **The National Archives**, although some are still 'closed' for the period after 1946.

The Imperial War Museum's Department of Printed Books holds published sources only, some of which are listed in Appendix V, but recommends in particular, the volumes of *Seedie's Rolls of Honour and Awards* published by Ripley Registers.

The Museum's Department of Documents holds a large collection of files relating to the Victoria Cross, which can be consulted by prior appointment. They also hold extensive collections of letters, personal papers and diaries, which sometimes mention awards made to naval personnel for specific actions.

For a fuller range of the awards available to personnel of the Royal Navy, please refer to the list of abbreviations in Appendix III. For information on the awards themselves, refer to the publications listed in Appendix V. Information on the Victoria Cross and George Cross can be found on the Imperial War Museum's web-site. Readers may also be interested to know that the Museum has a gallery devoted to the Victoria Cross and George Cross. This includes the medals awarded to Jack Cornwell, the boy seaman who was the youngest naval recipient of the VC.

CASUALTY RECORDS

Casualty records are held by the **Ministry of Defence** departments and agencies, but microfilmed copies are also available for public consultation at **The National Archives**.

Deaths aboard ship of all officers and ratings are recorded in ships' Musters and Pay Books, so it is necessary to know the name of the ship and the approximate date of death in order to find the entry. The records at **The National Archives** are to be found in Admiralty files *ADM 242* and *ADM 104*.

Part of *ADM 242* consists of a card index giving the date, place and cause of death of all officers who died during the period 1914-1920. Included is a War Graves Roll for ratings who died during the period 1914-1919. These entries are arranged alphabetically and include rank, service number, name of vessel, date and place of birth, date and cause of death, location of the grave and address of the next-of-kin.

Registers of those killed and wounded for the period 1854-1929, including the First World War, and reports of deaths for the period 1939-1948, are to be found in *ADM 104*. Index volumes are available. These files are also arranged as described above but include a little more detail on the cause of death.

In addition, casualty records of Royal Naval Reserve officers for the period 1939-1946 are to be found in the Board of Trade files, *BT 164*.

In the case of the Royal Marines the '75-year restriction' applies, although some references are to be found in the Admiralty files *ADM 104*, covering the period 1939-1948.

Casualty listings of Royal Navy officers and ratings of the Royal Navy are also to be found in the following editions of the *Navy List*: July 1915; January and July 1916; April and July 1917 and July 1918.

Although the Imperial War Museum was not the official repository for casualty records, the Department of Printed Books does have some Royal Naval Division Casualty Ledgers. We have undertaken the task of transferring much of the original cut-and-paste sheaves of names to computer, supplemented by research in the Commonwealth War Graves Commission registers. The listings for Howe, Hood, Nelson, Drake, Anson and Hawke Battalions can be consulted in our Reading Room.

Additionally, the Department holds copies of two important typescript listings, *Names of Officers who Died during the Period beginning 3rd September 1939 and ending 30th June 1948* and the *Register of Deaths (Naval Ratings), 3rd September 1939 to 30th June 1948*. Copied from the original sets held by the Royal Naval Museum at Portsmouth, the Museum has arranged for these to become openly available through our public service. Service personnel are filed alphabetically by surname. The information given includes the Port Division and, in the case of ratings, the official number, followed by branch of service, ship or unit, date and place of birth, cause, date and place of death and, occasionally, details of decorations and any further notes. Department of Printed Books staff are happy to check whether a relative's name appears in the listing or, alternatively, the volumes can be consulted by prior appointment in our Reading Room.

Please note that the date and cause of death of officers and ratings during the First World War, in or out of service, is almost always entered in the individual service register, maintained by the Admiralty from the mid-nineteenth century onwards and now at **The National Archives**.

THE COMMONWEALTH WAR GRAVES COMMISSION

The **Commonwealth War Graves Commission, 2 Marlow Road, Maidenhead, Berkshire SL6 7DX** holds details of the burial place or commemoration site for all those who died in service during the periods 1914-1921 and 1939-1947.

This organisation was established in May 1917 as the Imperial War Graves Commission, but changed its name in 1960. It was decided that all service personnel would be treated equally, being buried close to where they died and with uniform headstones. These graves would be cared for in perpetuity. Those who had no known grave would have their names carved on a memorial.

As well as having information on the site of burial or place of commemoration, the Commission has details of when service personnel died and the unit to which they were attached at the time of death. Often details of their home address and next of kin were included. A series of registers records the names of naval officers and ratings who were 'buried at sea' during the First and Second World Wars and commemorated on the large naval memorials at, for instance, Chatham, Plymouth,

Portsmouth, Liverpool, Lowestoft and Lee-on-the-Solent. It is not possible to visit the Commonwealth War Graves Commission in person. The Commission may charge a search fee for postal enquiries, but since information is now computerised, it can be accessed freely via their *Debt of Honour* database available on their web-site: **www.cwgc.org** Copies of all the Commission's published registers are located in the Department of Printed Books' Reading Room and are in regular use.

Details of naval personnel buried in 'non-world war' graves are available from the **Armed Forces Personnel Administration Agency (JPAC), Joint Casualty and Compassionate Centre, Building 182, Royal Air Force Innsworth, Gloucester GL3 1HW**. Please mark your enquiry 'Memorials and Graves'.

PUBLISHED CASUALTY LISTS AND ROLLS OF HONOUR

In addition to the set of Commonwealth War Graves Commission memorial and cemetery registers, the Department of Printed Books holds a large collection of operational and unit histories, some of which include casualties, and a number of published rolls of honour. Of particular importance for confirming basic details are the two volumes of the *Cross of Sacrifice* by SD and DB Jarvis, which cover naval personnel. The information these volumes contain includes full name, rank, decorations, cause of death, date of death, unit and details of grave or memorial location. The authors have also taken care to cross-refer possible misspellings of names. Both the CWGC registers and the volumes of Jarvis are available on open access in our Reading Room. Extensive research conducted by volunteers taking advantage of our facilities has also resulted in the publication of two registers for Royal Marines who died in both world wars.

Our library catalogues contain numerous privately published rolls of honour for schools, universities, companies, professions, and localities. Local histories can be very informative. For instance, *Portsmouth and the Great War* edited by William Gates and published by the Evening News and Hampshire Telegraph in 1919, contains an extensive roll of honour and list of awards. Also noteworthy are the volumes of the *National Roll of the Great War 1914-1918* for Southampton and Portsmouth (Sections IV and X respectively). The National Roll project was never completed and is far from comprehensive. Inclusion was by subscription, and individuals listed included many combatants who survived the war. Although we have few comprehensive rolls of honour for individual ships, one notable holding is a listing for those lost on HMS *Hood* during the Second World War. Full details of all these titles appear in the **Select Bibliography**.

The **United Kingdom National Inventory of War Memorials**, based at the Imperial War Museum, may be able to assist with enquiries concerning memorials for Royal Naval personnel. The UKNIWM is an information-gathering project, which has created a database of all known war memorials in the United Kingdom, estimated to be in the region of seventy thousand. The database can be accessed at **www.ukniwm.org.uk** from November 2005. The UKNIWM (in conjunction with Channel 4) is currently working on a searchable index of names from the First World War, and this should also be available in November. Files containing additional material may be consulted in the UKNIWM office by prior appointment. The database can currently be consulted by appointment in the Reading Room. The National Inventory will welcome information on any memorial currently missing from their records.

ADDITIONAL SOURCES

SHIP AND CAMPAIGN HISTORIES

Campaign, unit and ships' histories will prove invaluable for background detail. The Department of Printed Books has, in the past few years, acquired photocopies of an extremely useful set of ships' histories compiled and held by the Ministry of Defence, Naval Historical Branch. These unpublished typescripts, providing a brief summary of service, have now largely been digitised and are expected to be available on our web-site from Autumn 2005. The amount of detail included varies according to when the vessel saw action. There is far more information on those vessels which saw service during the Second World War. Researchers interested in the Second World War may benefit from referring to these ships' histories in conjunction with the multi-volume *The War at Sea: Preliminary Narrative*, an unpublished typescript compiled by the Historical Section of the Admiralty during the war, which is also available in our Reading Room. The various published official histories can also be excellent sources of information. Some of these volumes have been republished by the Department of Printed Books and details can be found in Appendix V.

Other official documentation, such as operational records, unit diaries and ships' logs can be found at **The National Archives**. The most relevant Admiralty files are *ADM 1*, *ADM 116* and *ADM 137* for First World War operational records and unit reports, and *ADM 1*, *ADM 116* and *ADM 199* for those issued during the Second World War. Convoy records for the Second World War are to be found in *ADM 199*, ships' logs in *ADM 53*, and submarine logs in *ADM 173*.

The Department of Printed Books holds a good collection of complementary published sources, including titles giving technical background to the ships, armament and training involved, as well as badges, uniforms, and medals. We have an extensive run of *Jane's Fighting Ships*, and other technical material. Reference sources such as *Dictionary of Disasters at Sea* and Colledge's *Ships of the Royal Navy* can help to establish basic facts on any ship. Ships' magazines and newsletters can also provide some illuminating details of life in the service and aboard ship. Our collection of autobiographies can provide unexpected references on diverse sections of the Navy. It should be stressed, however, that the activities of naval personnel based ashore are difficult to trace; published material does tend to concentrate on front line actions. Warlow's *Shore Establishments of the Royal Navy* is useful for working out where a relative might have served on land. Only a small sample of useful titles can be included in the **Select Bibliography** in Appendix V.

Researchers are welcome to use any of the **Imperial War Museum's** collections by appointment. The six collecting departments of the Museum are: Art, Documents, Exhibits and Firearms, Film and Photograph Archives, Printed Books and the Sound Archive. The Department of Documents holds personal diaries and letters which may refer to a relative's ship, or to an action in which the ship was involved. In many cases the Photograph Archive can produce a print of an individual ship.

An access guide to all the Imperial War Museum collections is available upon request, and most departmental catalogues can be consulted as part of the **Collections Online** initiative on the Imperial War Museum web-site at

www.iwmcollections.org.uk   Not every item in the Museum has been catalogued on computer, and there will inevitably be some omissions, so please make enquiries with the relevant department if you do not find what you are looking for.

For those of you who wish to experience the dimensions and surroundings of a ship at first hand, a visit to HMS *Belfast*, opposite the Tower of London, should not be missed. This Second World War cruiser also saw service in Korea. Exhibitions on board show its history and depict naval life. If you are interested in finding out more about HMS *Belfast*, details of John Wingate's recently updated history of the Ship can be found in the **Select Bibliography**.

For information relating to the nineteenth century and earlier, we recommend contacting both the **Royal Naval Museum** and the **National Maritime Museum**. Details of these and other relevant museums and archives are outlined in Appendix IV.

PERIODICALS

Amongst the many service newspapers and journals held by the Department of Printed Books is the *Navy News*, published by the **Royal Naval Association**. This carries a column for contacting and tracing information on ex-servicemen.

Other service or ex-service journals and newsletters may offer a similar service. The Department of Printed Books currently receives over 500 periodical titles relating to the Museum's subject field, and can advise on those most relevant to a particular enquiry. The **Royal British Legion, 48 Pall Mall, London SW1Y 5JY** may also be a useful contact.

GENEALOGICAL SOURCES

In addition there are many magazines on the market which offer advice and guidance on family history. The Imperial War Museum has subscribed to *Family Tree Magazine* since 1989, (back copies can be consulted in our Reading Room), but there have been many new publications of this sort produced in recent years. *Family Tree Magazine* is published monthly by **ABM Publishing, 61 Great Whyte, Ramsey, Huntingdon, Cambridgeshire PE26 1HJ**. Other titles include *Family History News and Digest* produced by the Federation of Family History Societies, *Genealogists Magazine* by the Society of Genealogists, *Ancestors* published by The National Archives and *Family History Monthly*. Contact details for all these can be found in Appendix IV.

Genealogical societies, such as the **Federation of Family History Societies, c/o FFHS Administrator, PO Box 2425, Coventry CV5 6YX** and the **Society of Genealogists, 14 Charterhouse Buildings, Goswell Road, London EC1M 7BA**, are also able to offer advice, as well as provide details of local societies and organisations. Both societies have also produced useful guides for the family historian, some of which are listed in Appendix V.

The Family and Local History Handbook, published annually, is full of genealogical and historical articles of interest to the beginner and experienced researcher alike. It also contains contact details for a wide variety of registrars of births, marriages and deaths, record offices, libraries, museums and societies.

An online listing of record repositories can be found at **www.nationalarchives.gov.uk/archon** *The National Register of Archives* – available online at **www.nationalarchives.gov.uk/nra** – will allow some searching of archival catalogues. Details about family and local history resources located in Public Libraries, together with contact details, can be found at **www.familia.org.uk**

The internet has revolutionised family history research, and there are many web-sites that can help, either with a specific subject, contacting individuals or appealing for information. Not everything that appears on the internet is current or correct information, and you should always check to see who has created the web-site and what their aim is. Some web-site addresses appear in Appendix IV, but you should be aware that web-sites sometimes just disappear, and that new ones are springing into life all the time. Following links from one site to another can often be a rewarding activity, if sometimes frustrating.

Family History fairs are held regularly around the country, and can be excellent places for both beginners and experienced researchers to find out what is available. The Imperial War Museum does sometimes participate in larger fairs, and also regularly has family history days in the Museum galleries. Visitors are welcome to come and ask questions, and staff are able to spend longer dealing with these than we are in the normal course of our work. The Museum web-site has details of the dates of these events.

APPENDIX I

ADMINISTRATION AND ORGANISATION

The ships, shore establishments, and men and women of the Royal Navy are traditionally administered by the Admiralty, now part of the tri-service Ministry of Defence.

For much of the twentieth century British ships were assigned to various stations around the world, such as the China Station, or the North America and West Indies Station. Each ship would usually spend several years on such a station, before returning home to decommission.

Ships serving together were divided into Squadrons and Flotillas, each under the command of a senior naval officer. These Squadrons and Flotillas normally comprised a certain type of ship, ie Battle (battleship) and Cruiser Squadrons and Destroyer and Submarine Flotillas. The sizes of these varied according to circumstances and requirements.

In addition to the Navy's seagoing vessels, various naval establishments and bases bore the letters HMS before the name and flew the White Ensign in the same way as a ship.

Naval depots were concerned with the maintenance and equipping of the ships and the training of personnel. Those entering the Navy as ratings were allocated a particular depot, shown by the letters which preceded their official number. On completion of training they were drafted to a specific ship.

When this ship's commission was completed they returned to the depot for re-drafting or for further training. Depots kept full records of all movements, promotions and achievements of the personnel under attachment, although day-to-day concerns and welfare were the responsibility of the commanding officers of the ships to which they had been drafted.

RANKS AND TITLES

COMMISSIONED OFFICERS

The highest rank in the Royal Navy is Admiral of the Fleet, which is equivalent to Field Marshal in the Army and Marshal of the Royal Air Force. Below this rank are Admirals, Vice-Admirals and Rear-Admirals. Executive Officers of these ranks are termed Flag Officers, because in accordance with tradition, they are entitled to fly a special flag.

Next in rank are Captains, certain of whom may be given a temporary rank of Commodore for the period they hold an appointment, such as command of certain squadrons or command of one of the naval barracks. Commodores are also entitled to fly a distinguishing swallow-tailed flag called a Broad Pennant.

Below Captains are Commanders, Lieutenant-Commanders, Lieutenants, Sub-Lieutenants, Midshipmen and Naval Cadets. Promotions to Officer are available to those ratings who show outstanding promise, particularly during wartime.

Officers who are not in the Executive (Seaman) Branch have a word or letter inserted in their title to show the duties on which they are engaged. Therefore, a commander in the Accountant Branch is called a Paymaster Commander; in the Engineering Branch a Commander (E) or Engineer Commander; in the Medical Branch a Surgeon Commander, etc.

WARRANT OFFICERS
Warrant Officers have special titles which show the particular duties in which they have specialised. Therefore the rating who specialises in gunnery becomes a Gunner on promotion to Warrant Officer; Seaman becomes a Boatswain; Engine-Room Artificer a Warrant Engineer.

NAVAL RATINGS
The senior ratings in the Royal Navy are Chief Petty Officers, then Petty Officers, Leading Seamen, Able Seamen, Ordinary Seamen and Boys.

Branches, other than the Seaman Branch have generally the same structure but different titles, for example in the Signalling Branch a Chief Petty Officer is called Chief Yeoman of Signals, under which there are Yeoman of Signals, Leading Signalman and Signalman.

Those who have the qualifications of skilled tradesmen generally have the title of Artificer in the particular technical branch to which they belong, ie in the Engineering Branch, senior ratings are Chief Engine-Room Artificers who have under them Artificers of different classes. In other technical branches tradesmen are described according to their trades, eg Chief Blacksmith and Chief Shipwright.

The two largest groups on board ship were the Seamen and the Stokers. In the first half of the twentieth century, when most ships used coal rather than oil for fuel, stoker complements were very large.

THE RESERVES

In peacetime, personnel would volunteer to serve for a certain period, and might volunteer for further service and obtain a pension. On leaving the Navy they became members of the **Royal Fleet Reserve**, and might be recalled in time of war. Additional wartime officers and ratings were provided by the **Royal Naval Reserve** and the **Royal Naval Volunteer Reserve**.

The **Royal Naval Reserve** consisted generally of officers and men who were employed in the Merchant Navy. Besides Executive Officers there were Accountant and Engineer Officers in this reserve. An important section of the Royal Naval Reserve was the **Trawler Section**, set up in 1911 to employ trawlers as minesweepers and patrol vessels with the experienced personnel required. Although abolished in 1921 as a separate section, the **Royal Naval Reserve Trawler Section** remained quite distinct from the Royal Naval Reserve proper and continued to employ fishermen. During the Second World War the **Royal Naval Patrol Service** also manned small motor or steam vessels for a variety of duties and recruited those who had experience of such craft. Officers of the Royal Naval Reserve had the ranks of Skipper Lieutenant, Chief Skipper and Skipper, recruited from those who had commanded steam or motor fishing vessels.

In 1903 the Naval Forces Act formed a **Volunteer Reserve** for the Royal Navy. Personnel of this **Royal Naval Volunteer Reserve** came from all walks of life. During peacetime they continued to carry out their civilian jobs, but in their spare time attended local training centres for instruction and for short periods trained with the fleet. Besides the Executive Branch there were the Air, Medical, Accountant, Engineer and Chaplains Branches. In addition there was a Special Branch into which officers with certain specialist qualifications ie languages, required by the Navy, could enter. The bulk of the officers recruited during wartime were granted temporary commissions in the Royal Naval Volunteer Reserve. There was also the **Royal Naval Volunteer (Wireless) Reserve** which trained personnel for service as Wireless Telegraphists and the **Royal Naval Auxiliary Sick Berth Reserve**, recruited from members of the St John Ambulance Brigade, to provide support for the sick bays and naval hospitals in times of war.

In 1958 the Royal Naval Volunteer Reserve amalgamated with the Royal Naval Reserve.

THE ROYAL MARINES

The Marines are a self-contained body administered by the Admiralty. Their history is an interesting one and well documented (see **Select Bibliography**).

They were designated **The Royal Marines** in 1802 but in 1855 took the title **Royal Marine Light Infantry**. In 1859 the **Royal Marine Artillery** was formed as a distinct Division. In 1923 the Royal Marine Light Infantry and the Royal Marine Artillery merged to form, again, the Royal Marines.

Royal Marine officers rank with Army officers of the same title, but their pay and entitlements remain as for the relevant Navy rank. Captains of HM ships rank above all officers under their command whether afloat or ashore:

COMPARATIVE TABLE

Royal Navy	Royal Marines	Army
Admiral of the Fleet	-	Field Marshal
Admiral	General	General
Vice-Admiral	Lieutenant-General	Lieutenant-General
Rear-Admiral	Major-General	Major-General
Commodore	Brigadier	Brigadier
Captain	Colonel	Colonel
Commander	Lieutenant-Colonel	Lieutenant-Colonel
Lieutenant-Commander	Major	Major
Lieutenant	Captain	Captain
Sub-Lieutenant	Lieutenant	Lieutenant
-	2nd Lieutenant	2nd Lieutenant

Other ranks also compare with the Army: Warrant Officer, Colour Sergeant, Sergeant, Corporal, Private (Royal Marines Light Infantry), Bombardier, Gunner, (Royal Marine Artillery). When both branches amalgamated in 1923, the ranks of Bombardier, Gunner and Private disappeared, the latter two being replaced by Marine. In addition, as the Marines are employed in specialist trades there are Marine Armourers, Marine Artificers, Marine Engineers; and since musicians entered service with the Royal Marine Bands: Bandmasters, Band Corporals, Buglers and Bandsmen.

Broadly speaking, the duties of the Marines have been the manning of guns for the Navy and landing as a striking force wherever the military situation demanded. However, some of these duties, and training, have changed with the times. The First World War saw the mobilisation of Reserves of the Royal Marines and they served in all theatres of war either on ships or ashore. Plans for a Mobile Naval Base Defence Organisation, to specialise in amphibious and raiding operations, were made shortly before the outbreak of the Second World War. From 1942 Royal Marine Commandos were established (not to be confused with Army Commandos which came into being in 1940 and had lower unit numbers); numbers 40-48 Commando were all Royal Marine units and operational in the Second World War.

ROYAL NAVAL DIVISION

The origins of the **Royal Naval Division (RND)** can be traced to Admiralty plans several years prior to the outbreak of war in 1914, to form an 'Advanced Base Force' of Royal Marines to seize and/or protect naval bases that might be required to re-inforce, protect or supply ground troops. When sent to assist the Ostend garrison in August 1914, the original Royal Naval Brigade had been strengthened by two brigades of Naval reservists. Their formation and subsequent history as a land force, first under the Admiralty and later under the War Office, is recorded in the history by Douglas Jerrold, entitled *The Royal Naval Division*. Rupert Brooke was probably its most famous son, but it 'attracted men of a remarkable quality'. Its membership was drawn not only from the Royal Marines and Royal Naval Volunteer Reserve (which provided the largest contingent), but from the Royal Fleet Reserve and newly-joined recruits taken over from the War Office – men who had enlisted mostly in the Durham Light Infantry, the Northumberland Fusiliers and the King's Own Yorkshire Light Infantry. They formed a remarkable unit which served on land throughout the war, but maintained the traditions and customs associated with the Navy. They grew beards, flew the White Ensign in their camps, and used nautical language; they adopted naval ranks, and were subject to naval pay and discipline. On 29 April 1916 the Division was transferred to the War Office and was redesignated the 63rd (Royal Naval) Division on 19 July. The Department of Printed Books is fortunate to hold a number of very useful sources on the Division. (See the **Select Bibliography** for details).

ROYAL NAVAL AIR SERVICE AND FLEET AIR ARM

The first Naval Air Department was set up in 1909 to build dirigibles. In 1911 a **Naval Wing** of the **Royal Flying Corps (RFC)** was established and 1912 saw the formation of the **Royal Naval Flying School** at Eastchurch.

In April 1914 regulations for a separate **Royal Naval Air Service (RNAS)** were issued and from July it was officially recognised, with all personnel to be borne on the books of HM ships and serving under the provisions of the Naval Discipline Act. At this time the Flying School passed to War Office administration.

In 1915 a complete reorganisation took place with all RNAS personnel coming under the control of the Admiralty, including all those in air stations. HMS *Daedalus* became the Central Depot while the Training Establishment was based at Cranwell. Up until this time the RNAS had been involved with home defence, anti-aircraft and searchlight units, armoured car squadrons and kite balloons, but when all 'non-naval' functions were passed to the Army, their roles were re-defined as coastal observers, interception of enemy aircraft over the sea, defence of naval centres and scouting for enemy submarines and minelayers.

During the First World War RNAS personnel held the ranks of their original branch, with the addition of the words Wing, Squadron, Flight and Observer. For example, Wing Commander, Squadron Commander, Flight Commander, Squadron Observer, Flight Observer, Flight Lieutenant, Observer Lieutenant, Flight Officer and Observer Officer. A full listing is to be found in the appropriate editions of the *Navy List*.

In November 1917 the Air Force (Constitution) Act was passed, amalgamating the **RNAS** with the **RFC** to form a new service, the **Royal Air Force (RAF)**, which was established in April 1918. All RNAS personnel working on airships or kite balloons were transferred to the RAF. The Airship Service was finally disbanded in 1921.

By 1918 the 'Air Service' had over 120 stations at home and abroad, with 67,000 personnel and 3,000 aircraft of all types, and had operated in all theatres during the First World War. However, from that date the Navy ceased to possess its own flying branch; although the observers and air gunners were naval, most of the pilots and all the maintenance crews were from the RAF. This inter-service rivalry regarding the control of naval aviation, continued throughout the inter-war period. Although an improved working relationship had been achieved by the end of the 1920s, it was not until 1937, after much political wrangling, that the Admiralty again took over responsibility for its own flying and the **Fleet Air Arm (FAA)** was formed, although it was not officially designated as such until 1953. (See **Select Bibliography** for recommended titles on Fleet Air Arm history).

THE COASTGUARD SERVICE

The **Coastguard** first functioned as a 'reserve' for the Royal Navy in 1856 when control was passed to the Admiralty. From that date, in addition to defending coastlines, protection of the revenue and the manning of the Royal Navy in time of war, the Coastguard was also responsible for assisting vessels in distress, lifesaving, searching for mines and torpedoes as well as duties connected with signalling, telegraphs, lighthouses and salvage.

Many Coastguards were former sailors and were called up during the First World War. Large numbers lost their lives in the earlier engagements and the remainder were brought home to guard the shores against enemy landings. Here their skills in signalling and telegraphy were deployed to relay messages between the Admiralty and the naval and merchant vessels. Despite a reduction in numbers after the war, the remainder were organised into a **Naval Signalling Section**, controlled by the Admiralty or were reorganised for coast watching and lifesaving, by the Board of Trade.

The two departments worked together during the 1930s and in 1939 auxiliary Coastguards were recruited on National Service, their key tasks being signalling and intelligence. However, in 1940 the Admiralty assumed control and armed the Coastguard. During the Second World War they were the first line of defence against threatened invasion. In 1945 after a reduction in auxiliary Coastguard numbers, the Service came under the control of the Ministry of Transport until 1964 when control reverted to the Department of Trade. Since then the main responsibility of the Coastguard has been search and rescue around the coast.

WOMEN'S SERVICES
The **Women's Royal Naval Service (WRNS or 'Wrens')** was originally created in 1917 and disbanded in 1919, but then reorganised in 1939. The WRNS became a permanent part of the Royal Navy in 1949.

The WRNS was originally set up to replace various categories of naval personnel in shore establishments. Its main purpose during the First and Second World Wars was to 'Free a man to join the Fleet.' It increasingly took over jobs and trades of a very specialist nature and served in naval barracks, stations and bases at home and abroad. It was only in 1977 that female officers and ratings became subject to the Naval Discipline Act. 1993 saw the disbandment of the WRNS, with women being totally integrated into the Royal Navy. They now hold the same rank, are paid the same salary and undertake the same duties as their male counterparts, except service in submarines and minor war vessels.

Officer ranks during the First World War were as follows: Director, Deputy Director, Assistant Director, Deputy Assistant Director, Divisional Director, Deputy Divisional Director, Principal, Deputy Principal, Assistant Principal. From 1939: Director, Deputy Director, Assistant Director, Superintendent, Chief Officer, 1st Officer, 2nd Officer, 3rd Officer.

Ratings ranks generally adopted, until recent times, were as follows: Chief Wren, Petty Officer Wren, Leading Wren, Wren.

NURSING SERVICES

Female nurses have been employed by the Navy since the seventeenth century, but a professional service was introduced in 1884 with the establishment of the **Naval Nursing Service**. Nursing Sisters first served on board hospital ships in 1897 with the Benin Expedition. Queen Alexandra, wife of King Edward VII, assumed patronage of the Naval Nursing Service in 1902 and it was renamed **Queen Alexandra's Royal Naval Nursing Service (QARNNS)**.

Although **Nursing Sisters** had the status of officers, it was only in 1977 that they became subject to the Naval Discipline Act and were formally commissioned. Ranks included: Matron-in-Chief, Matron, Superintending Sister, Nursing Sister, Sister, Head Nurse and Nurse. From 1960 a two tier organisation was established, with nurses ranked as ratings. In 1983 men became eligible to join QARNNS. In April 2000, QARNNS was incorporated into the Royal Navy as the service's discrete nursing specialisation.

During both world wars the nursing service was supplemented by civilian nurses, such as **VADs (Voluntary Aid Detachments)** organised through the Red Cross. Although many VADs volunteered for wartime duties during the First World War, only a small proportion actually served with the Navy. A much higher proportion served during the Second World War. When the VADs were mobilised again in 1939, they began to replace Sick-Berth staff who had been drafted to ships.

Another important role was to provide female nursing care wherever members of the WRNS were employed, including service abroad. After the war ended many VADs continued to serve and in 1949 a **Voluntary Aid Detachment Reserve** was formed. The same year saw the formation of the Sick-Berth rating category of the WRNS. VADs were given the option of retaining their separate identity or joining the newly formed WRNS Branch, which continued until 1960 when it was subsumed, along with the remaining VADs, by **Queen Alexandra's Royal Naval Nursing Service**.

APPENDIX II

OFFICIAL NUMBERING

From 1873 all ratings of every branch of the Navy, already in service, were allocated an 'official number'. Every type of new entrant to the Navy would in future be given such a number. The organisation and development of this system is rather complex and deserves more in-depth study, but outlined below are descriptions of the main aspects of the system, such as the allocation of blocks of numbers and the differing prefix and/or suffix letters to denote the branch, specialist duty, type of entry, home port, differing pay scales and length of service in the Navy.

The Admiralty decided that the first block of official numbers, 40,001 up to 178,000, would be allocated to all ratings irrespective of their branch of service. In 1894 a more specialised block number allocation system was introduced, differentiating between branches of ratings. A new system was introduced in 1908 using four prefix letters to denote groups of branches:

	1894	1908
Seamen and Communications Ratings	178,001 – 240,500	J. 1 – 115,433
Engine Room Artificers	268,001 – 273,000	M. 1 – 39,555
Stokers	276,001 – 313,000	K. 1 – 66,973
Artisans and Miscellaneous	340,001 – 348,000	M. 1 – 39,555
Sick-Berth Staff and Ships' Police	350,001 – 352,000	M. 1 – 39,555
Stewards, Cooks and Boy Servants	353,001 – 366,450	L. 1 – 15,101

These numbers with branch prefix letters were used throughout the First World War until a revised pay code was introduced for new entrants in 1925. Since the Admiralty wished to distinguish between those on the new pay code and those on the old pay code, all new entrants had the letter **X** added to their prefix, with the following blocks of numbers:

Seamen	J.X. 125,001-
Stokers	K.X. 75,001-
Stewards and Cooks	L.X. 20,001-
Miscellaneous	M.X. 45,001-

The use of the letter **X** continued until 1953.

In 1894 the Admiralty had decided that all entrants to the Navy should be appropriated to one of the three Manning Ports – Chatham, Devonport or Portsmouth – according to the locality in which they may have been recruited. All ratings were to belong to their designated port for the duration of their service. The letters used were **C**, **D** and **P** for Chatham, Devonport and Portsmouth and from 1914, **F** for the **Royal Naval Air Service**, later **Fleet Air Arm**. Although these letters formed part of the ratings' official identification, it was not until 1934 that it was decreed that the Port Division letter appear immediately before the official number.

In 1943 another new numbering system was introduced, starting with 500,000. All entrants were to retain their official number, even if they changed their branch. Only the prefix letters changed. Letters **J**, **K**, **L**, **M** and **F** were retained for normal engagements and **SS**, **SK**, **SL**, **SM**, and **SF** introduced for special service engagements. A further allocation of numbers was issued to new entrants in 1953. These comprised a six figure number, starting with 000,001 prefaced by three letters (without spaces or punctuation). These letters referred to Port Division, Type of Engagement and Branch:

Port Divisions: **C** for Chatham; **D** for Devonport; **E** for Malta; **G** for Trincomalee; **L** for Lee-on-Solent; **LT** for Lowestoft; **N** for Nore; **P** for Portsmouth and **R** for Rosyth.

Engagements: **C** for Continuous Service; **N** for National Service; **S** for Special Service and **T** for Temporary Service. **H** was kept for possible use during 'Hostilities Only'.

Branches: **A** for Artificers; **B** for Sick-Berth; **C** for Cooks; **D** for Coders; **E** for Electrical Branch; **J** for Seamen, Signalmen and Telegraphists; **K** for Engineering Mechanics; **N** for Airmen and Aircraft Mechanics; **Q** for Stores; **R** for Regulating Staff; **V** for Stewards; **W** for Writers and **Z** for Artisans.

In 1957 a central drafting system was introduced and individual port drafting offices were superseded, consequently the Port Division letters were dropped. In 1959, a new and simplified system was introduced for all entrants. The new official starting number became 050,001, prefixed with a single letter to indicate the rating's selected depot or 'Welfare Authority'.

Officers are issued with service numbers primarily for pay and administrative reasons, and these numbers are usually prefixed by the letter **C**.

No published accounts specifically on the official numbering system in the **Royal Navy** are available. More detailed records on this subject can be found at **The National Archives**.

APPENDIX III

ABBREVIATIONS

These are a selection only of the most commonly used abbreviations. A fuller listing is to be found in all editions of the *Navy List* (a near complete run from 1914 to date is held by the Department of Printed Books). In addition, the Department holds several published guides to abbreviations in use at various times during the twentieth century.

GENERAL

ADM	Admiralty
CG	Coastguard
CS	Continuous Service
CWGC	Commonwealth War Graves Commission
FAA	Fleet Air Arm
HM	His Majesty's/Her Majesty's
HMS	His Majesty's Ship/Her Majesty's Ship
IWGC	Imperial War Graves Commission
MAC	Merchant Ship Aircraft Carrier
MOD	Ministry of Defence
NA	National Archives (formerly the Public Record Office)
NAAFI	Navy, Army and Air Force Institute
NATO	North Atlantic Treaty Organisation
PRO	Public Record Office (renamed The National Archives in 2003)
QARNNS	Queen Alexandra's Royal Naval Nursing Service

RAF	Royal Air Force
RAN	Royal Australian Navy
RCN	Royal Canadian Navy
RCNC	Royal Corps of Naval Constructors
RFA	Royal Fleet Auxiliary
RFC	Royal Flying Corps
RFR	Royal Fleet Reserve
RM	Royal Marines
RMA	Royal Marine Artillery
RMLI	Royal Marine Light Infantry
RMO	Reserve of Medical Officers
RN	Royal Navy/Royal Naval
RNA	Royal Naval Academy
RNAS	Royal Naval Air Service/ Royal Naval Air Station
RNAWR	Royal Naval Auxiliary Wireless Reserve
RNC	Royal Naval College
RNEC	Royal Naval Engineering College
RND	Royal Naval Division
RNH	Royal Naval Hospital
RNPS	Royal Naval Patrol Service
RNR	Royal Naval Reserve
RNR(T)	Royal Naval Reserve Trawler Section
RNTS	Royal Naval Transport Service
RNVR	Royal Naval Volunteer Reserve
RNV(S)R	Royal Naval Volunteer Supplementary Reserve
RNV(W)R	Royal Naval Volunteer Wireless Reserve
RNXS	Royal Naval Auxiliary Service
TNA	The National Archives (formerly the Public Record Office)
VAD	Voluntary Aid Detachments/ Voluntary Aid Detachment

WRNR	Women's Royal Naval Reserve
WRNS	Women's Royal Naval Service

RANKS AND TITLES

A	Admiral
AF	Admiral of the Fleet
ASL	Acting Sub-Lieutenant
B	Boatswain
Bndr	Bandmaster, Royal Marines
C	Captain
Cd	Commissioned
Cdr	Commander
Cdre	Commodore
Cdt	Cadet
Ch	Chaplain
C-in-C	Commander-in-Chief
CO	Chief Officer
CPO	Chief Petty Officer
Cr	Commander
E Cr	Engineer Commander
El L	Electrical Lieutenant
ERA	Engine Room Artificer
FO	Flag Officer
FONAC	Flag Officer Naval Air Command
Gr	Gunner
Hon L	Honorary Lieutenant
L	Lieutenant
L Col	Lieutenant-Colonel, Royal Marines
L Cr	Lieutenant-Commander
Lt	Lieutenant

Lt Col	Lieutenant-Colonel, Royal Marines
Lt Cdr	Lieutenant-Commander
Mid	Midshipman
OL	Ordnance Lieutenant
P Cr	Paymaster Commander
PO	Petty Officer
Pres Ch	Presbyterian Chaplain
RA	Rear-Admiral
Schm	Schoolmaster
Sen Mr	Senior Master
Sg C	Surgeon Captain
SH L	Shipwright Lieutenant
Sig L	Signal Lieutenant
Skr	Skipper
SL	Sub-Lieutenant
TL	Telegraphist Lieutenant
VA	Vice-Admiral
W Eng	Warrant Engineer
Wg Cdr	Wing Commander
Wt	Warrant

HONOURS AND AWARDS

AFC	Air Force Cross
ARRC	Associate of the Order of the Royal Red Cross
BEM	British Empire Medal
CB	Companion of the Order of the Bath
CBE	Commander of the Order of the British Empire
CGM	Conspicuous Gallantry Medal
Commendn	Commendation

DCM	Distinguished Conduct Medal
DFC	Distinguished Flying Cross
DSC	Distinguished Service Cross
DSM	Distinguished Service Medal
DSO	Companion of the Distinguished Service Order
GC	George Cross
GM	George Medal
KBE	Knight Commander of the Order of the British Empire
KCB	Knight Commander of the Order of the Bath
KG	Knight of the Order of the Garter
LS & GCM	Long Service and Good Conduct Medal
MBE	Member of the Order of the British Empire
MC	Military Cross
MID	Mention in Despatches
MM	Military Medal
MSM	Meritorious Service Medal
OBE	Officer of the Order of the British Empire
RRC	Member of the Order of the Royal Red Cross
RRC Bar	Bar to the Royal Red Cross
VC	Victoria Cross

APPENDIX IV

ADDRESSES

Listed below are details of some additional museums, archives and record offices, which may be able to offer further assistance with family history enquiries. Please note that it is always advisable to contact an institution in advance of an intended visit, in order to check on the availability of material relating to your particular enquiry and confirm opening hours. Most of the Ministry of Defence departments and agencies will only deal with enquiries by post. Those with Internet access will find that many institutions now have their own web-site, which outlines their holdings, arrangements for public access and details of any search fees and/or charges which may be levied. Information on other museums and archives is to be found in such annual publications as the *World of Learning* and the *Museums Yearbook*, available at most libraries and information centres. Aslib, in collaboration with the Museums Association, also publishes the very useful *Directory of Museums and Special Collections in the United Kingdom*.

MINISTRY OF DEFENCE OFFICES

Most Ministry of Defence departments and agencies operate a postal service only (see section on **Service Records** for details of coverage).

Armed Forces Personnel Administration Agency (JPAC)

Joint Casualty and Compassionate Centre   Building 182, Royal Air Force Innsworth, Gloucester GL3 1HW

Armed Forces Personnel Administration Agency
MOD Medal Office Building 250, Royal Air Force Innsworth, Gloucester
GL3 1HW

DPS(N) (Directorate of Personnel Support (Navy))
Building 1/152, Victory View, HM Naval Base, Portsmouth,
Hampshire PO1 3PX

Naval Secretary (Honours and Awards)
Victory Building, HM Naval Base, Portsmouth, Hampshire PO1 3LS

Navy Search
TNT Archive Services, Tetron Point, William Nadin Way, Swadlincote,
Derbyshire DE11 0BB

RECORD OFFICES

Commonwealth War Graves Commission
2 Marlow Road, Maidenhead, Berkshire SL6 7DX
Tel: 01628 634221
www.cwgc.org

Family Records Centre
1 Myddelton Street, London EC1R 1UW
Tel: 020 8392 5300
www.familyrecords.gov.uk/frc/

General Register Office
PO Box 2, Southport, Merseyside PR8 2JD
Tel: 0845 603 7788
www.gro.gov.uk

General Register Office (Dublin)
Government Offices, Covent Road, Roscommon, Eire
Tel: 090 6632900
www.groireland.ie

General Register Office (Northern Ireland)
Oxford House, 49-55 Chichester Street, Belfast, Northern Ireland BT1 4HL
Tel: 028 9025 2000
www.groni.gov.uk

General Register Office for Scotland
New Register House, Edinburgh, Scotland EH1 3YT
Tel: 0131 334 0380
www.gro-scotland.gov.uk/

The National Archives
Ruskin Avenue, Kew, Richmond, Surrey TW9 4DU
Tel: 020 8876 3444
www.nationalarchives.gov.uk

National Archives of Ireland
Bishop Street, Dublin 8, Eire
Tel: 03531 407 2300
www.nationalarchives.ie

National Archives of Scotland
HM General Register House, 2 Princes Street, Edinburgh, Scotland EH1 3YY
Tel: 0131 535 1334
www.nas.gov.uk

Public Record Office of Northern Ireland
66 Balmoral Avenue, Belfast, Northern Ireland BT9 6NY
Tel: 028 9025 5905
www.proni.gov.uk

MUSEUMS, LIBRARIES AND ARCHIVES

British Empire and Commonwealth Museum
Clock Tower Yard, Temple Meads, Bristol BS1 6QH
Tel: 0117 925 4980
www.empiremuseum.co.uk

British Library, Newspaper Library
Colindale Avenue, London NW9 5HE
Tel: 020 7412 7353
www.bl.uk/collections/newspapers.html

British Red Cross Museum and Archives
44 Moorfields, Moorgate, London EC2Y 9AL
Tel: 020 7877 7000
www.redcross.org.uk

Fleet Air Arm Museum
Centre for Naval Aviation Records and Research, Box D6, RNAS Yeovilton,
Yeovil, near Ilchester, Somerset BA22 8HT
Tel: 01935 840565
www.fleetairarm.com

Guildhall Library
Aldermanbury, London EC2P 2EJ
Tel: 020 7332 1868
www.cityoflondon.gov.uk/search_guildhall

**Hull City Museums, Art Galleries and Archives
(Maritime Museum)**
c/o Ferens Art Gallery, Queen Victoria Square, Hull HU1 3RA
Tel: 01482 613902
www.hullcc.gov.uk/museums

Lowestoft and East Suffolk Maritime Museum
Sparrows Nest Gardens, Whapload Road, Lowestoft, Suffolk NR32 1XG
Tel: 01502 561963

Merseyside Maritime Museum
Albert Dock, Liverpool L3 4AQ
Tel: 0151 4784499
www.liverpoolmuseums.org.uk

National Library of Wales
Aberystwyth, Ceredigion, Wales SY23 3BU
Tel: 01970 632800
www.llgc.org.uk

QARNNS (Queen Alexandra's Royal Naval Nursing Service)
Archive
Institute of Naval Medicine
Alverstoke, Gosport, Hampshire PO12 2DL

National Maritime Museum
Romney Road, Greenwich, London SE10 9NF
Tel: 020 8858 4422
www.nmm.ac.uk

Plymouth Naval Studies Collection
City of Plymouth Libraries and Information Service, Drake Circus, Plymouth,
Devon PL4 8AL
Tel: 01752 305909
www.plymouth.gov.uk

Portsmouth Museums and Records Service
Museum Road, Portsmouth, Hampshire PO1 2LJ
Tel: 023 9282 7261
www.portsmouthcitymuseums.co.uk

Royal Air Force Museum

Grahame Park Way, Hendon, London NW9 5LL

Tel: 020 8205 2266

www.rafmuseum.org.uk

Royal Marines Museum

Southsea, Hampshire PO4 9PX

Tel: 023 9281 9385

www.royalmarinesmuseum.co.uk

Royal Naval Museum

HM Naval Base (PP66), Portsmouth, Hampshire PO1 3NH

Tel: 023 9272 7562

www.royalnavalmuseum.org

Royal Navy Submarine Museum

HMS Dolphin, Haslar Jetty Road, Gosport, Hampshire PO12 2AS

Tel: 023 9252 9217

www.rnsubmus.co.uk

Southampton City Archives

Southampton City Council, South Block, Civic Centre,

Southampton SO14 7LY

Tel: 023 8083 2251

www.southampton.gov.uk/leisure/archives/

Wellcome Library (for the History and Understanding of Medicine)

210 Euston Road, London NW1 2BE

Tel: 020 7611 8722

www.wellcome.ac.uk

Women's Library
Old Castle Street, London E1 7NT
Tel: 020 7320 2222
www.thewomenslibrary.ac.uk

ASSOCIATIONS

Association of Wrens
8 Hatherley Street, London SW1P 2YY
Tel: 020 7932 0111
www.wrens.org.uk

Navy News
HMS *Nelson*, Leviathan Block, Portsmouth, Hampshire PO1 3HH
Tel: 023 9229 4228
www.navynews.co.uk

QARNNS Association [officers and ratings]
Institute of Naval Medicine, Alverstoke, Gosport, Hampshire PO12 2DL

Royal British Legion
48 Pall Mall, London SW1Y 5JY
Tel: 08457 725 725
www.britishlegion.org.uk

Royal Naval Association Headquarters
82 Chelsea Manor Street, London SW3 5QJ
Tel: 020 7352 6764
www.royal-naval-association.co.uk

Royal Naval Patrol Service Association
Sparrows Nest Gardens, Whapload Road, Lowestoft, Suffolk NR32 1XG
Tel: 01502 586250
www.rnps.lowestoft.org.uk

V.A.D. (R.N.) Association
Institute of Naval Medicine, Alverstoke, Gosport, Hampshire PO12 2DL

GENEALOGY

Ancestors
PO Box 38, Richmond, TW9 4AJ
www.ancestorsmagazine.co.uk

Family History Monthly
The Metropolis Group, 140 Wales Farm Road, London W3 6UG
Tel: 0870 732 8080

Family Tree Magazine
61 Great Whyte, Ramsey, Huntingdon, Cambridgeshire PE26 1HJ
Tel: 01487 814050
www.family-tree.co.uk

Federation of Family History Societies
FFHS Administrator, PO Box 2425, Coventry CV5 6YX
[publishes *Family History News and Digest*]
www.ffhs.org.uk

Practical Family History
61 Great Whyte, Ramsey, Huntingdon, Cambridgeshire PE26 1HJ
Tel: 01487 814050
www.family-tree.co.uk

Society of Genealogists
14 Charterhouse Buildings, Goswell Road, London EC1M 7BA
[publishes *Genealogists Magazine*]
Tel: 020 7251 8799
www.sog.org.uk

ADDITIONAL WEB-SITES

ARCHON (Archives Online)
www.nationalarchives.gov.uk/archon

Association of Royal Navy Officers
www.eurosurf.com/ARNO

Britain's Small Wars, 1945-2003
www.britains-smallwars.com

Familia: the UK and Ireland's Guide to Genealogical Resources in Public Libraries
www.familia.org.uk

Family Records.gov.uk Consortium
www.familyrecords.gov.uk

Fleet Air Arm Archive
www.fleetairarmarchive.net

Forces Reunited
www.forcesreunited.org.uk

Gazettes-Online
www.gazettes-online.co.uk

GENUKI: UK & Ireland Genealogy

www.genuki.org.uk

Marine Society

www.marine-society.org

Maritime and Coastguard Agency

www.mcga.gov.uk

Maritime Britain

www.maritimebritain.org.uk

MOD Reunited

www.modreunited.com

National Register of Archives

www.nationalarchives.gov.uk/nra

Naval Historical Collectors and Research Association

www.nhcra-online.org

Naval History (site by Gordon Smith)

www.naval-history.net

PORT: Maritime Information Gateway

www.port.nmm.ac.uk

Royal Marines Regimental Site

www.royalmarinesregimental.co.uk

Royal Navy

www.royal-navy.mod.uk

SSAFA Forces Help

www.ssafa.org.uk

Submariners Association

www.submarinersassociation.co.uk

All contact details in this publication were correct at the time of printing.

APPENDIX V

SELECT BIBLIOGRAPHY

Below are listed a selection of published sources and material held by the Department of Printed Books. These may be consulted in our Reading Room by prior appointment; please give at least 24 hours notice of arrival. In addition, specific short subject bibliographies and information sheets are available on request. Please note that we have not attempted to list the many periodical titles that are relevant to naval research, but we are happy to advise on specific titles where applicable.

Many of these recommended publications will also be available though your local public library or bookseller and in the case of the 'out of print' volumes through second-hand and specialist dealers.

For ease of use, the list has been broken down into the following main subject areas to reflect the different sections in this booklet: Genealogy, Family History, Service Records and Archival Guides (p. 69); Medals and Awards (p. 71); Casualties and Rolls of Honour (p. 74); Naval Operations in the Twentieth Century (p. 77); Histories of the Royal Navy and its Ships (p. 81); Life and Customs in the Royal Navy (p. 87).

GENEALOGY, FAMILY HISTORY, SERVICE RECORDS AND ARCHIVAL GUIDES

The National Archives have produced a series of helpful leaflets on a variety of subjects. These can be found on their web-site **www.catalogue.nationalarchives.gov.uk**

ADMIRALTY
Navy List: containing Lists of Ships, Establishments and Officers of the Fleet...
Admiralty, London, 1898-
[Serial publication]

BECKETT, Ian FW
The First World War: the Essential Guide to Sources in the UK National Archives by Ian FW Beckett.
Public Record Office, Richmond, Surrey, 2002.
ISBN 1-903365-41-4

BEVAN, Amanda
Tracing your Ancestors in the Public Record Office by Amanda Bevan.
6th rev. ed.; Public Record Office, Richmond, Surrey, 2002.
(Public Record Office Handbook; no. 19)
ISBN 1-903365-34-1 (pbk.)

BLATCHFORD, Robert
The Family and Local History Handbook: incorporating the Genealogical Services Directory edited and compiled by Robert Blatchford.
8th ed.; Robert Blatchford Publishing, York, 2004.
ISBN 0-95302977-8 (pbk.)

CANTWELL, JD

The Second World War: a Guide to Documents in the Public Record Office by John D Cantwell.

3rd rev. ed.; Public Record Office, Richmond, Surrey, 1998.

(Public Record Office Handbook; no. 15)

ISBN 1-873162-60-X (pbk.)

COLWELL, Stella

The Family Records Centre: a User's Guide by Stella Colwell.

Public Record Office, Richmond, Surrey, 2002.

(Public Record Office Readers' Guide; no. 17)

ISBN 1-903365-36-8 (pbk.)

COX, Jane

New to Kew?: a first time Guide for Family Historians at the Public Record Office, Kew by Jane Cox.

Public Record Office, Richmond, Surrey, 1997.

(Public Record Office Readers' Guide; no. 16)

ISBN 1-873162-40-5 (pbk.)

FOSTER, Janet

British Archives: a Guide to Archive Resources in the United Kingdom edited by Janet Foster and Julia Sheppard.

4th ed.; Palgrave Publishers, Basingstoke, Hampshire, 2002.

ISBN 0-333-73536-6

PAPPALARDO, Bruno

Tracing your Naval Ancestors by Bruno Pappalardo.

Public Record Office, Richmond, Surrey, 2003.

(Public Record Office Readers' Guide; no. 24)

ISBN 1-903365-37-6 (pbk.)

RODGER, NAM

Naval Records for Genealogists by NAM Rodger.

Public Record Office, Richmond, Surrey, 1998.

(Public Record Office Handbook; no. 22)

ISBN 1-873162-58-8 (pbk.)

THOMAS, Garth

Records of the Royal Marines by Garth Thomas.

Public Record Office, Richmond, Surrey, 1994.

(Public Record Office Readers' Guide; no. 10)

ISBN 1-87316-219-7 (pbk.)

MEDALS AND AWARDS

ABBOTT, PE

British Gallantry Awards by PE Abbott and JMA Tamplin.

Nimrod Dix, London, 1981.

ISBN 0-902633-74-0

CREAGH, O'Moore

The VC and DSO: a Complete Record of all those Officers, Non-Commissioned Officers and Men of His Majesty's Naval, Military And Air Forces who have been Awarded these Decorations from the Time of their Institution... edited by the late Sir O'Moore Creagh (until 1920) and EM Humphris, with a foreword by Earl Beatty, Earl of Cavan and Sir HM Trenchard.

Standard Art Book, London, [1924].

DICKSON, Bill Chatterton

Seedie's List of Coastal Forces Awards for World War II compiled by Bill Chatterton Dickson.

Ripley Registers, Tisbury, Wiltshire, 1992.

ISBN 0-9513380-3-X

DICKSON, Bill Chatterton
Seedie's List of Fleet Air Arm Awards, 1939-1969 compiled by Bill Chatterton Dickson.
Ripley Registers, Tisbury, Wiltshire, 1990.
ISBN 0-9513380-2-1

DICKSON, Bill Chatterton
Seedie's List of Submarine Awards for World War II compiled by Bill Chatterton Dickson.
Ripley Registers, Tisbury, Wiltshire, 1990.
ISBN 0-9513380-1-3

DICKSON, Bill Chatterton
Seedie's Roll of Naval Honours and Awards, 1939-1959 compiled by Bill Chatterton Dickson.
Ripley Registers, Tisbury, Wiltshire, 1989.
ISBN 0-9513380-0-5

DORLING, H Taprell
Ribbons and Medals by H Taprell Dorling; edited and revised by Alec A Purves.
Osprey, London, 1983.
ISBN 0-85045-516-2

DYMOND, Steve
Researching British Medals: a Practical Guide by Steve Dymond.
Crowood Press, Marlborough, Wiltshire, 1999.
ISBN 1-86126-282-5

FEVYER, WH
The Distinguished Service Cross, 1901-1938 by WH Fevyer.
London Stamp Exchange, London, 1991.
ISBN 0-948130-63-6

FEVYER, WH
The Distinguished Service Medal, 1914-1920 compiled by WH Fevyer.
Hayward, London, 1982.
ISBN 0-903754-97-5

FEVYER, WH
The Distinguished Service Medal, 1939-1946 compiled by WH Fevyer.
Hayward, London, 1981.
ISBN 0-903754-90-8

GOULD, Robert W
British Campaign Medals: Waterloo to the Gulf by Robert W Gould.
4th rev. ed.; Arms and Armour Press, London, 1994.
ISBN 1-85409-224-3

MORRIS, Kenneth DOUGLAS-
Naval Long Service Medals, 1830-1990 by Kenneth Douglas-Morris.
[privately printed], London, 1991.

Naval and Air Force Honours and Awards: [reprinted from the Navy List and Air Force List, 1919-1920].
Hayward, London, [1974].
ISBN 0-903754-07-X

The Register of the Victoria Cross.
Rev. ed.; This England Books, Cheltenham, 1988.
ISBN 0-906324-07-6

WINTON, John
The Victoria Cross at Sea by John Winton.
Michael Joseph, London, 1978.
ISBN 0-7181-1701-8

CASUALTIES AND ROLLS OF HONOUR

SHIPS' LOSSES

British Vessels Lost at Sea, 1914-18 and 1939-45:
[facsimile reprints of four HMSO official publications]...
Patrick Stephens, Wellingborough, Northants., 1988.
ISBN 1-85260-134-5

HOCKING, Charles
Dictionary of Disasters at Sea during the Age of Steam..., 1824-1962 [2 volumes]
by Charles Hocking.
Lloyd's, London, 1969.

HOOKE, Norman
Modern Shipping Disasters, 1963-1987 by Norman Hooke.
Lloyd's, London, 1989.
ISBN 1-85044-211-8

YOUNG, John M
Britain's Sea War: a Diary of Ship Losses, 1939-1945 by John M Young.
Patrick Stephens, Wellingborough, Northants., 1989.
ISBN 1-85260-042-X

MEMORIALS

GIBSON, Edwin
Courage Remembered: the Story Behind the Construction and Maintenance of the
Commonwealth's Military Cemeteries and Memorials of the Wars of 1914-1918
and 1939-1945 by Edwin Gibson and G Kingsley Ward.
HMSO, London, 1989.
ISBN 0-11-772608-7

SAUNDERS, David

Britain's Maritime Memorials and Mementoes by David Saunders.
Patrick Stephens, Sparkford, Somerset, 1996.
ISBN 1-85260-466-2

ROLLS OF HONOUR

ADMIRALTY

*Names of Officers who Died during the Period beginning 3rd September 1939
and ending 30th June 1948.*
Admiralty, London, 1939-1948.
Photocopy held by Department of Printed Books of original typescript held
by the Ministry of Defence, Naval Historical Branch.

ADMIRALTY

*Official Communiqué announcing the following Casualties sustained in HMS
Hood...*
Admiralty, London, 1941.

ADMIRALTY

Register of Deaths (Naval Ratings), 3 September 1939 to 30 June 1948.
Admiralty, London, 1939-1948.
The Department of Printed Books holds a photocopy of the original eight
volume set of typescript sheets.

GATES, William G

Portsmouth and the Great War edited by William G Gates.
Evening News and Hampshire Telegraph, [Portsmouth], 1919.
Includes roll of honour.

GOOD, JA
A Register of Royal Marines War Deaths, 1939-1945 compiled by JA Good.
Royal Marines Museum, Southsea, Hants., 1986-1987.

HMS Hood Roll of Honour.
N.pub., n.p., [199-?].
Presented to the Imperial War Museum by the Founder of the HMS Hood
Association.

JARVIS, SD
Cross of Sacrifice. Volume 2: Officers who Died in the Service of the Royal Navy, Royal Naval Reserve, Royal Naval Volunteer Reserve, Royal Marines, Royal Naval Air Service and Royal Air Force, 1914-1919 by SD Jarvis and DB Jarvis.
Roberts Medals, Reading, Berkshire, 1993.
ISBN 1-873058-31-4

JARVIS, SD
Cross of Sacrifice. Volume 4: Non-commissioned Officers, Men and Women of the United Kingdom, Commonwealth and Empire who Died in the Service of the Royal Navy, Royal Marines, Royal Naval Air Service and Royal Air Force, 1914-1921: including the Commonwealth Navies and Air Forces by SD Jarvis and DB Jarvis.
Roberts Medals, Reading, Berkshire, 1996.
ISBN 1-873058-41-1

National Roll of the Great War.
National Publishing, London, [1920-1922?]
Especially, Section IV: Southampton, and Section X: Portsmouth

ROYAL MARINES HISTORICAL SOCIETY
With Full and Grateful Hearts: a Register of Royal Marines Deaths, 1914-1919.
Royal Marines Historical Society, Southsea, Hants., 1991.

WAVE HERITAGE TRUST

The Royal Naval Volunteer Reserve: Roll of Honour, 1939-1945.
Wave Heritage Trust, London, 2001.

MEDICAL

MELLOR, W Franklin
Casualties and Medical Statistics edited by W Franklin Mellor.
HMSO, London, 1972.
(History of the Second World War. United Kingdom Medical Series)
ISBN 0-11-320997-5

MITCHELL, TJ
Medical Services: Casualties and Medical Statistics of the Great War by TJ Mitchell
and Miss GM Smith.
HMSO, London, 1931.
(History of the Great War based on Official Documents)
[The Imperial War Museum, Department of Printed Books produced a
reprint of this volume in 1997 with the ISBN 1-870423-28-3]

NAVAL OPERATIONS IN THE TWENTIETH CENTURY

GENERAL WORKS

ALBION, Robert Greenhalgh
Naval and Maritime History: an Annotated Bibliography by Robert Greenhalgh
Albion.
4th ed.; David and Charles, Newton Abbot, Devon, 1973.
ISBN 0-7153-6007-8

LABAREE, Benjamin Woods

A Supplement (1971-1986) to Robert G Albion's Naval and Maritime History: an Annotated Bibliography by Benjamin W Labaree.

4th ed.; Mystic Seaport Museum, Mystic, Connecticut, 1988.

ISBN 0-913372-46-3 (pbk.)

FIRST WORLD WAR

CORBETT, Julian S

Naval Operations [5 volumes and 4 map cases] by Sir Julian S Corbett and Sir Henry Newbolt.

Longmans, Green, London, [1920-1931].

(History of the Great War based on Official Documents)

[The Imperial War Museum, Department of Printed Books produced reprints of these volumes between 1995 and 1997, and paperback reprints became available in 2004]

GIBSON, RH

The German Submarine War, 1914-1918 by RH Gibson and Maurice Prendergast.

Constable, London, 1931.

[A paperback reprint became available in 2003]

MARDER, Arthur J

From the Dreadnought to Scapa Flow: The Royal Navy in the Fisher Era, 1904-1919: [5 volumes] by Arthur J Marder.

Oxford University Press, London, 1961-1970.

ISBN 0-19-215187-8

THOMPSON, Julian

The Imperial War Museum Book of the War at Sea 1914-1918 by Julian Thompson.

Sidgwick and Jackson, London 2005.

ISBN 0-283-07354-3

SECOND WORLD WAR

ADMIRALTY. NAVAL STAFF. TACTICAL TORPEDO AND STAFF DUTIES DIVISION

The War at Sea, September 1939-September 1945: Preliminary Narrative prepared by the Admiralty Naval Staff, Tactical, Torpedo and Staff Duties Division.

Admiralty, London, 1944-1946.

BARNETT, Correlli

Engage the Enemy more closely: the Royal Navy in the Second World War by Correlli Barnett.

Hodder and Stoughton, London, 1991.

ISBN 0-340-33901-2

HAGUE, Arnold

The Allied Convoy System, 1939-1945: its Organization, Defence and Operation by Arnold Hague.

Chatham Publishing, London, 2000.

ISBN 1-86176-147-3

LAW, Derek G

The Royal Navy in World War Two: an Annotated Bibliography by Derek G Law.

Greenhill Books, London, 1988.

ISBN 1-85367-002-2

RICHARDS, Brooks

Secret Flotillas [two volumes] by Brooks Richards.

2nd ed.: Frank Cass, London, 2004.

ISBN 0-7146-5316-0

[originally published by HMSO in 1996]

ROHWER, Jürgen

Allied Submarine Attacks of World War Two: European Theatre of Operations, 1939-1945 by Jürgen Rohwer.

Greenhill Books, London, 1997.

ISBN 1-85367-274-2

ROHWER, Jürgen

Axis Submarine Successes, 1939-1945 by Jürgen Rohwer.

Patrick Stephens, Cambridge, 1983.

ISBN 0-85059-695-5

ROSKILL, SW

The War at Sea, 1939-1945 [4 volumes] by SW Roskill.

HMSO, London, [1954-1961].

(History of the Second World War. United Kingdom Military Series)

[Paperback reprint became available in 2004]

THOMPSON, Julian

The Imperial War Museum Book of the War at Sea: the Royal Navy in the Second World War by Julian Thompson.

Sidgwick and Jackson, London, 1996.

ISBN 0-283-06252-5

HISTORIES OF THE ROYAL NAVY AND ITS SHIPS

ADMIRALTY AND ORGANISATION

GARDINER, Leslie
The British Admiralty by Leslie Gardiner.
Blackwood, Edinburgh, 1968.
ISBN 0-85158-001-7

WARLOW, B
Shore Establishments of the Royal Navy: being a List of the Static Ships and Establishments of the Royal Navy compiled by B Warlow.
Maritime Books, Liskeard, Cornwall, 2000.
ISBN 0-907771-73-4

SHIPS

COLLEDGE, JJ
Ships of the Royal Navy: the Complete Record of all Fighting Ships of the Royal Navy by JJ Colledge; revised by Ben Warlow.
Rev. ed.: Greenhill Books, London, 2003.
ISBN 0-85367-566-0

Conway's all the World's Fighting Ships 1906-1921.
Conway Maritime Press, London, 1985.
ISBN 0-85177-245-5

Conway's all the World's Fighting Ships 1922-1946.
Conway Maritime Press, London, 1980.
ISBN 0-85177-146-7

Conway's all the World's Fighting Ships 1947-1995.
Conway Maritime Press, London, 1995.
ISBN 0-85177-605-1

Jane's Fighting Ships
Jane's Yearbooks, London
Annual publication.
Printed Books holdings include volumes from 1898-date (incomplete).

WINGATE, John
In Trust for the Nation: HMS Belfast, 1939-1972 by John Wingate.
Rev. ed.; Imperial War Museum, London, 2004.
ISBN 1-901623-72-6

ROYAL MARINES

BLUMBERG, HE
Britain's Sea Soldiers: a Record of the Royal Marines During the War 1914-1919
by HE Blumberg.
Swiss, Devonport, 1927.

FRASER, Edward
The Royal Marine Artillery, 1804-1923 [2 volumes] by Edward Fraser and LG
Carr-Laughton.
Royal United Service Institution, London, 1930.

LADD, James D
By Sea, by Land: the Royal Marines, 1919-1997: an Authorised History by James
D Ladd.
Rev. ed.; HarperCollins, London, 1998.
ISBN 0-00-472366-X

THOMPSON, Julian
The Royal Marines: from Sea Soldiers to a Special Force by Julian Thompson.
Sidgwick and Jackson, London, 2000.
ISBN 0-283-06315-7

NAVAL RESERVES

BOWEN, Frank C
History of the Royal Naval Reserve by Frank C Bowen.
Lloyd's, London, 1926.

KERR, J Lennox
The RNVR: a Record of Achievement by J Lennox Kerr and Wilfred Granville.
Harrap, London, 1957.

RNR 100: Celebrating 100 Years: Centenary of the Naval Volunteer Reserves [1903-2003].
Benham Publishing, Liverpool, 2003

ROYAL NAVAL DIVISION

The Collingwood Battalion, Royal Naval Division: a Short History of the Collingwood Battalion in the Dardanelles together with Biographical Notes of all the Officers and a List of the Men compiled by Lieut. Stanley Geary, RM
2nd ed.; FJ Parson (printers), Hastings, [1919?]

JERROLD, Douglas
The Hawke Battalion: some Personal Records of Four Years, 1914-1918 by Douglas Jerrold.
Ernest Benn, London, 1925.

JERROLD, Douglas
The Royal Naval Division by Douglas Jerrold.
2nd ed.; Hutchinson, London, 1927.

The Mudhook: the Journal of the 63rd (R.N.) Division.
[Printed Books holds all ten issues produced between 1917 and 1919]

RND Royal Naval Division: Antwerp, Gallipoli and France 1914–1918.
Quarterly journal issued by L Sellers since 1997, which contains in-depth articles and research.

PAGE, Christopher
Command in the Royal Naval Division: a Military Biography of Brigadier General AM Asquith, DSO by Christopher Page.
Spellmount, Staplehurst, Kent, 1999.
ISBN 1-86227-048-1

SELLERS, Leonard
The Hood Battalion, Royal Naval Division: Antwerp, Gallipoli, France 1914-1918 by Leonard Sellers.
Leo Cooper, London, 1995.
ISBN 0-85053-386-9

SPARROW, Geoffrey
On Four Fronts with the Royal Naval Division by Geoffrey Sparrow, MC, and JN Macbean Ross, MC.
Hodder and Stoughton, London, 1918.

NAVAL AVIATION

KING, Brad
Royal Naval Air Service, 1912-1918 by Brad King; edited by Barry Ketley.
Hikoki Publications, Aldershot, 1997.
ISBN 0-9519899-5-2

STURTIVANT, Ray
British Naval Aviation: the Fleet Air Arm, 1917-1990 by Ray Sturtivant.
Arms and Armour, London, 1990.
ISBN 0-85368-938-5

STURTIVANT, Ray
Fleet Air Arm Aircraft, Units and Ships, 1920 to 1939 by Ray Sturtivant with Dick Cronin.
Air Britain (Historians), Tonbridge, Kent, 1998.
ISBN 0-85130-271-8

STURTIVANT, Ray
The Squadrons of the Fleet Air Arm by Ray Sturtivant.
Air Britain (Historians), Tunbridge Wells, Kent, 1984.
ISBN 0-85130-120-7

AUXILIARY SERVICES

BOWSER, Thekla
The Story of British VAD Work in the Great War by Thekla Bowser.
Andrew Melrose, London, [1917].
[The Imperial War Museum, Department of Printed Books produced a reprint of this volume in 2003 with the ISBN 1-901623-60-2]

COULTER, JLS

The Royal Naval Medical Service [2 volumes] by JLS Coulter.
HMSO, London, 1954-1956.
(History of the Second World War. United Kingdom Medical Series.)

HARLAND, Kathleen

A History of Queen Alexandra's Royal Naval Nursing Service by Kathleen Harland.
Journal of the Royal Naval Nursing Service, Portsmouth, 1990.
ISBN 0-9514906-0-5 (pbk.)

TAYLOR, CM

Nursing in the Senior Service, 1902-2002: Personal Histories of Queen Alexandra's Royal Naval Nursing Service edited by CM Taylor.
QARNNS Association, Gosport, 2002.
ISBN 0-9541646-0-1 (pbk.)

WEBB, William

Coastguard!: an Official History of HM Coastguard by William Webb.
HMSO, London, 1976.
ISBN 0-11-510675-8

WOMEN'S ROYAL NAVAL SERVICE

FLETCHER, MH

The WRNS: a History of the Women's Royal Naval Service by MH Fletcher.
Batsford, London, 1989.
ISBN 0-7134-6185-3

MASON, Ursula Stuart
Britannia's Daughters: the Story of the WRNS by Ursula Stuart Mason.
Leo Cooper, London, 1992.
ISBN 0-85052-271-4

THOMAS, Lesley
WRNS in Camera by Lesley Thomas and Chris Howard Bailey.
Sutton, Stroud, Gloucestershire, 2002.
ISBN 0-7509-1370-3

LIFE AND CUSTOMS IN THE ROYAL NAVY

ADMIRALTY. NAVAL TRAINING DEPARTMENT
Naval Ratings Handbook by the Admiralty, Naval Training Department.
Admiralty, London, 1951.
[The Imperial War Museum, Department of Printed Books produced a reprint of this volume in 2002 with the ISBN 1-901623-57-2 (pbk.)]

BURNS, KV
Badges and Battle Honours of HM Ships by KV Burns.
Maritime Books, Liskeard, Cornwall, 1986.
ISBN 0-907771-26-2

CAMPBELL, AB
Customs and Traditions of the Royal Navy: with Chapters on the Royal Marines, the Women's Royal Naval Service, Naval Decorations and Medals by AB Campbell.
Gale and Polden, Aldershot, 1956.

HAMPSHIRE, A Cecil
Just an Old Navy Custom by A Cecil Hampshire.
Kimber, London, 1979.
ISBN 0-7183-0486-1

KEMP, Peter

The British Sailor: a Social History of the Lower Deck by Peter Kemp.
Dent, London, 1970.

LAVERY, Brian

Hostilities Only: Training the Wartime Royal Navy by Brian Lavery.
National Maritime Museum, London, 2004
ISBN 0-948065-48-6

M^cKEE, Christopher

Sober Men and True: Sailor Lives in the Royal Navy, 1900-1945
Harvard University Press, Cambridge, Massachusetts, 2002
ISBN 0-674-00736-0

POOLMAN, Kenneth

The British Sailor by Kenneth Poolman.
Arms and Armour, London, 1989.
ISBN 0-85368-992-X

SMITH, Peter C

Royal Navy Ships' Badges by Peter C Smith.
Photo Precision, St Ives, Huntingdon, 1974.
ISBN 0-85944-011-7

THOMAS, David A

Battles and Honours of the Royal Navy by David A Thomas.
Leo Cooper, London, 1998.
ISBN 0-85052-623-X

WELLS, John

The Royal Navy: an Illustrated Social History, 1870-1982 by Captain John Wells.
Sutton, Stroud, Gloucestershire, 1994.
ISBN 0-7509-0524-7

RESEARCH FACILITIES AT THE IMPERIAL WAR MUSEUM

THE READING ROOM

Formerly the chapel of the Bethlem Royal Hospital, or Bedlam, this historic room is used extensively by authors, scholars, journalists, broadcasters and visitors alike. Readers have access to a major reference library of printed materials encompassing everything from trench maps to a vast journals collection. The Department of Documents holds an extensive collection of unpublished diaries, letters and memoirs of servicemen and women and civilians.

Access to the Reading Room is free but you should make an appointment in advance.

Monday – Saturday 10.00am-5.00pm
Closed: Bank Holiday weekends, 24, 25, 26 December and for a period of 2 weeks (usually May) for stocktaking purposes

When making an appointment please give us as much detail of your area of research as possible. Material can then be pre-selected and ready on your arrival. However, this should not deter you from a further catalogue search of your own. We will be happy to show you the various catalogues and options open to you. Bags are not generally allowed in the reading room – these should be left in the cloakroom – although handbags and portable computers are admissible. Please remember that this is an old building and, although we have done much to improve the provision of electric points, lighting and ventilation, we are limited by the amount of physical space actually available. We will, however, always try to accommodate anyone wishing to consult our collections. The design limitations of this building make access to the Reading Room difficult for many disabled visitors but alternative facilities are available. Please ask when making your appointment.

Photocopying and other services
Guidance on photocopying procedures is available in printed form in the Reading Room itself. We are bound by the copyright law, and by our own conservation and preservation requirements. Black and white photocopies are available at a fixed Museum price and special photography can be arranged. Booklists and information sheets are available on a variety of subjects.

Our contact details:

Department of Printed Books
Imperial War Museum, Lambeth Road, London SE1 6HZ
Tel: 020 7416 5342 (for general enquiries and appointments)
Fax: 020 7416 5246
E-mail: books@iwm.org.uk

Department of Documents
Imperial War Museum, Lambeth Road, London SE1 6HZ
Tel: 020 7416 5222
Fax: 020 7416 5374
E-mail: docs@iwm.org.uk

Other Collecting Departments
[all postal enquiries should be addressed to the appropriate department at Imperial War Museum, Lambeth Road, London SE1 6HZ]

Department of Art
Material may be seen by prior appointment in the Print Room at the Museum's Lambeth Road branch, Tuesday-Thursday, 10.00am-5.00pm. To arrange a visit, contact the Department's Research and Information Officer.
Tel: 020 7416 5211
E-mail: art@iwm.org.uk

Department of Exhibits and Firearms
A visitor's room is open by appointment, Monday-Friday, 10.00am-5.00pm.
Tel: 020 7416 5272 / 5304 / 5305
Fax: 020 7416 5374
E-mail: exfire@iwm.org.uk

Film and Photograph Archives

The Film Archive is open by appointment from Monday-Friday, 10.00am-5.00pm. At least 24 hours notice is normally sufficient to research the catalogue, but 5-7 days notice is required to view any film selected. Film viewing and handling fees are charged. The Visitor's Room is located at: All Saints Annexe, Austral Street, London SE11.
Tel: 020 7416 5291 / 5292
Fax: 020 7416 5299
E-mail: film@iwm.org.uk

The Photograph Archive Visitors' Room at the All Saints Annexe, Austral Street, is open to visitors, by appointment, from Monday-Friday, 10.00am-5.00pm.
Tel: 020 7416 5333 / 5338 [Please allow a minimum of 24 hours notice]
Fax: 020 7416 5355
E-mail: photos@iwm.org.uk

Sound Archive

The Visitors Room at the All Saints Annexe, Austral Street is open by appointment, Monday to Friday, 10.00am-5.00pm. Visitors may listen to tapes and consult printed and database catalogues; some typescripts available.
Tel: 020 7416 5363
E-mail: sound@iwm.org.uk

Collections Online

An exciting new development has been the launch of **Collections Online** at **www.iwmcollections.org.uk**
The initial tranche of material was made public in 2002, and catalogues from all the Collecting Departments were made

available in 2004. For the first time you can access the Museum's catalogues on-line. If you want to browse there are short essays on major historical themes, which lead you to selected highlights from all over the collections, including artworks, documents, exhibits, film, photographs and sound recordings. Currently 160,000 records are available, although it is important to realise that no catalogue is ever totally complete – if you don't find what you are looking for, please contact us and ask.

GENERAL CONTACTS

The Museum has five branches. These are:

Imperial War Museum London
Lambeth Road, London SE1 6HZ
Open daily, 10.00am-6.00pm
Tel: 020 7416 5000 / 5320 (general enquiries)
Fax: 020 7416 5374
E-mail: mail@iwm.org.uk

Churchill Museum and Cabinet War Rooms
Clive Steps, King Charles Street, London SW1A 2AQ
Open daily
Summer (1 April-30 September) 9.30am-6.00pm
last admission 5.15pm
Winter 10.00am-6.00pm, last admission 5.15pm
Tel: 020 7930 6961
Fax: 020 7839 5897
E-mail: cwr@iwm.org.uk

HMS *Belfast*

Morgan's Lane, Tooley Street, London SE1 2JH
Open daily
Summer (1 March-31 October) 10.00am-6.00pm,
last admission 5.15pm
Winter 10.00am-5.00pm, last admission 4.15pm
Tel: 020 7940 6300
Fax: 020 7403 0719
E-mail: hmsbelfast@iwm.org.uk

Imperial War Museum Duxford

Cambridgeshire CB2 4QR
Open daily
Summer (mid March-mid October) 10.00am-6.00pm,
last admission 5.15pm
Winter 10.00am-4.00pm, last admission 3.15pm
Tel: 01223 835000
Fax: 01223 837267
E-mail: duxford@iwm.org.uk

Imperial War Museum North

The Quays, Trafford Wharf, Trafford Park,
Manchester M17 1TZ
Open daily
Summer (1 March-31 October) 10.00am-6.00pm,
last admission 5.30pm
Winter 10.00am-5.00pm, last admission 4.30pm
Tel: 0161 836 4000
Fax: 0161 836 4012
E-mail: iwmnorth@iwm.org.uk

All branches are closed 24, 25, 26 December

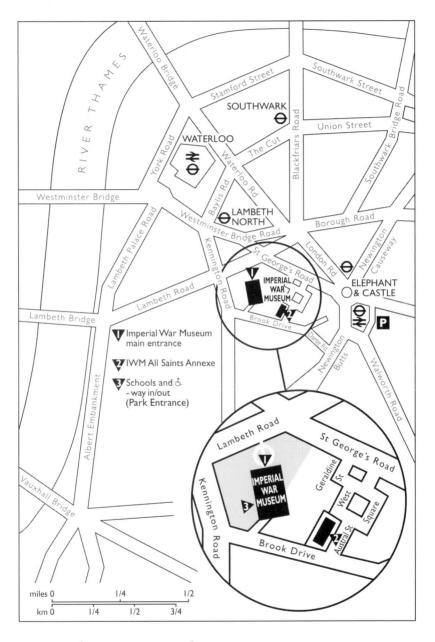

www.iwm.org.uk